DEVELOPING
AND USING TESTS
EFFECTIVELY

LUCY CHESER JACOBS
CLINTON I. CHASE

DEVELOPING
AND USING TESTS
EFFECTIVELY

A
GUIDE
FOR
FACULTY

Jossey-Bass Publishers · San Francisco

For sales outside the United States contact Maxwell Macmillan
International Publishing Group, 866 Third Avenue, New York,
New York 10022.

Manufactured in the United States of America

The paper used in this book is acid-free and meets the
State of California requirements for recycled paper
(50 percent recycled waste, including 10 percent
postconsumer waste), which are the strictest guidelines
for recycled paper currently in use in the United States.

Library of Congress Cataloging-in-Publication Data

Jacobs, Lucy Cheser.
    Developing and using tests effectively : a guide for faculty /
Lucy Cheser Jacobs, Clinton I. Chase. — 1st ed.
        p.   cm. — (The Jossey-Bass higher and adult education series)
    Includes bibliographical references (p.   ) and index.
    ISBN 1-55542-481-3 (alk. paper)
    1. Universities and colleges—United States—Examinations—Design
and construction.   I. Chase, Clinton I.   II. Title.   III. Series.
LB2366.2.J33   1992
378.1'661—dc20   92-19335
                                                    CIP

The Bach fugue on p. 78 is from p. 238 of *Materials and Structure of Music*
(2nd ed.) by W. Christ, R. DeLone, V. Kliewer, and others (1973) and
appears courtesy of Prentice Hall.

FIRST EDITION
HB Printing   10 9 8 7 6 5 4 3 2   *Code 9280*

The Jossey-Bass
Higher and Adult Education Series

Contents

Contents

Preface

Professor Ecks is three weeks into the semester in his American history class, and it is time for an assessment of how well the students are fulfilling the course objectives. But writing and scoring tests are such dull, even frustrating tasks. The fun part is teaching, not testing!

Surrounded by textbooks and government archival documents, he clears a space on his desk and takes out a legal-size tablet. He opens the course textbook and thumbs through some of the reading assignments looking for items that could go into a test, items that are not so obvious that everybody might have learned the answers. As he skims through the text, he scribbles down a list of topics and specific relevant points — grist for test making.

"Hmm! Shall I write a bunch of multiple-choice items — or maybe true-false? They're easy to write." He glances at the clock — 5:15 P.M. "Well, the secretary is gone; have to type these things myself." He scratches the stubble on his cheek as he mulls over the options. "Oh, hold it!" he thinks, "I could combine some of these topics into essay questions — make those kids think for a while. I only need about five or six questions if I use essay — and they'll be easy to type — An essay test it is!"

Professor Ecks begins: "Item 1. List the names and dates of two battles in the Civil War that took place north of the Mason-Dixon Line, and discuss their importance.

"Item 2. Discuss . . . ."

The plight of Professor Ecks is not unlike that of many teachers we have encountered in our role of testing center directors. His plan has no systematic structure, nothing tying test type or content to course objectives, and no clear guidelines for item construction. The procedures are adapted to the exigencies of the moment, not to assessment policy. How many times we have seen this script played out!

Indeed, most faculty members report to us that they do not like to write tests, score tests, or report test results to their students. They hate to be hassled by students who think a test item was ambiguous or claim that the instructor misinterpreted what was written. Furthermore, faculty tell us that they feel less than competent in developing tests and have little technical skill in managing the problems they encounter in the testing operation. It is situations like these that have led us to write *Developing and Using Tests Effectively*.

Evaluation is a time-consuming function at most colleges. After talking with hundreds of faculty members at the college level, we estimate that up to 20 percent of a professor's time is spent evaluating the impact of instruction. Yet most teachers come to that task with little formal training in how to select a testing procedure, how to construct a test well, or how to deal with it after it has been constructed. As a result, they fall back on the procedures they experienced as students and often make the same mistakes that they complained about their professors' making.

Purpose

Because we believe that there is much more to good testing than any one of us ourselves has learned from taking tests as a student, we designed this book to help faculty members write better classroom tests. There are sound principles and techniques for testing that faculty can quickly learn and apply to test preparation. Of course, preparing good tests involves more than following a set of rules. It requires creativity, originality, knowledge of the material, and practice. But following the principles of test construction can make the task easier and help instructors produce good tests faster than they could with the "hard knocks" system.

We also want faculty to acquire a new perspective on the benefits of classroom testing. Teachers tend to view tests primarily as a basis for course grades and seem not to be aware of the impact that tests have on the overall quality of students' learning and instructors' teaching. Students adapt to teachers' focus on the obtainment of scores rather than on the learning that testing can provide. We think faculty members want to be better evaluators of student learning; the ideas, plans, and procedures contained in this book will be helpful to both beginning faculty and experienced instructors for developing better assessment systems and applying them more effectively.

Background and Audience

The book grew out of our years of experience as college teachers and as administrators at a university testing center. We have had many opportunities to help faculty for whom testing was a new or troublesome experience. During the many workshops and other presentations we have offered, faculty members have shared their concerns about testing and grading, including their anxieties about facing their classes with the tests they had prepared. Most faculty sincerely want to be excellent teachers, but they often lack the resources to improve their skills.

In our workshops, serious interest is expressed in improving classroom tests. At the same time, faculty have many misconceptions about types of tests and about testing procedures in general. We think that capable teachers should be informed about all aspects of classroom technique, including testing. *Developing and Using Tests Effectively* is a step in the direction of helping faculty members expand their ability to assess learning outcomes.

Most of the literature on testing and measurement consists of textbooks designed to prepare teachers for elementary and secondary schools. Because we know of no other recent books on testing that have been written strictly for college instructors, we decided to provide a practical, concise book just for busy faculty. In addition, it will serve as a handy, readable reference for faculty and instructional developers.

Overview of the Contents

The chapters are arranged in a sequence similar to that one follows in planning, constructing, and administering a classroom test. Readers may want to proceed through the chapters in order, or they may want to read only selected chapters that provide the information they want. The first three chapters provide background information. In Chapter One, we discuss the importance of course exams to both instructors and students and introduce a number of terms commonly used to describe tests.

Good tests require planning for the methods of administration and assessment, the content of the test, and the handling of results. Chapter Two focuses on the planning that goes into constructing a good classroom test. We stress the importance of writing instructional objectives whose attainment can be observed and measured. We introduce Bloom's taxonomy as a particularly useful device for classifying the cognitive objectives to be measured in most college courses. We also discuss several decisions that have to be made before the test is developed and provide guidelines for decision making.

All measurements, including tests, have to meet certain technical requirements before the data yielded can be considered trustworthy. Chapter Three discusses the extremely important concepts of validity—the extent to which a test relates to course content—and reliability—the degree to which a test is a consistent measure of achievement. Any test must have these two qualities to be useful in making decisions about students or about instruction. Although both are technical characteristics, we do not overwhelm the readers with statistical details. Instead, we focus on the factors that are known to affect the validity and reliability of classroom tests, factors that are under the control of the instructor.

Because postsecondary courses vary widely in their setup and objectives, assessment of instructional outcomes requires an array of techniques. Our next four chapters deal with the actual writing of different types of test items. Chapter Four looks at the widely used multiple-choice format. But just a minute, here. Aren't multiple-choice tests limited to basic facts and bits of trivia? We think not, and we show that multiple-choice items can be written to measure attainment of higher-level cognitive objectives. Not only do we describe the procedure for measuring skills such as analysis, application, and evaluation but we also illustrate the results with items from different disciplines.

Chapter Five expands the instructor's view of testing techniques and provides a variety of procedures to increase the instructor's versatility as an evaluator. The chapter deals with objective items (other than multiple-choice) that can be used in the college classroom, including true-false, matching, and completion items.

Writing skill is an important objective of the college curriculum, and many faculty see it as a means of assessing students' cognitive development. Chapter Six examines essay tests, another test format widely used in college classrooms. We discuss when essay tests should be used and give guidelines for preparing and scoring essay questions. We also look at the limitations of essay tests and offer suggestions for helping students write better essays.

The commonly used testing procedures will be seen by some faculty members as less than satisfactory. To some of our colleagues, conventional testing just lacks a real-life component. They may have experimented with unique approaches to assessment that fit their particular needs and found that the outcomes showed merit. In Chapter Seven, we describe a few of the nontraditional testing procedures, such as performance tests and take-home, open-book, and oral examinations, discussing their advantages and limitations. We also look at the alternatives offered by multiple testing, portfolios, and project approaches.

Now that we have given instructors a wide range of assessment types from which to choose, the next step is administering the test, the subject of Chapter Eight. Proper administration is extremely important, because the way a test is administered can affect its validity and reliability. Also in this chapter, we discuss cheating and suggest ways to deal with the problem.

This is the electronic age, and testing is increasingly computerized. In Chapter Nine, instructors are introduced to computer-assisted testing. We try to lay out the most common approaches, along with some of the advantages and complications.

Once instructors have written a test and administered it to their class, they wonder how successfully the test discriminates between students of high and low achievement. That depends on how well the test items individually are working—the subject of Chapter Ten. We include suggestions using item analysis to improve test-writing skills.

After administering a test and scoring it, college instructors spend hours stewing over assigning grades to students. In our experience, most faculty members have no substantial guidelines for devising a grade distribution system and consequently feel rather insecure in their effort to rank students on a grade scale. With no firm guidance, instructors prefer to err on the side of leniency rather than harshness. Grade inflation is the result.

In Chapter Eleven, we outline the general principles that should guide grading in the college classroom and give teachers a more defensible basis for assigning grades. We also discuss how to weight various types of student data for the final grade and how to come up with grading categories.

We undertook to write this book because in our experience, faculty often are quite unfamiliar with the variety of techniques that go into assessment of learning outcomes. We feel certain that faculty who seriously study the contents of this book will become more skilled and confident in their assessment of student achievement. Moreover, *Developing and Using Tests Effectively* will indirectly help students, because the tests it influences will be used as learning aids as well as fair and reasonable measuring devices. At any rate, that is our objective, and we believe that we have presented the material in a way that should help college teachers become as proficient in assessment as they are in other aspects of their craft. If indeed they achieve that goal, we will have met ours.

Bloomington, Indiana   Lucy Cheser Jacobs
August 1992   Clinton I. Chase

The Authors

Lucy Cheser Jacobs is director of the Bureau of Evaluative Studies and Testing at Indiana University, Bloomington. She received her B.S. degree (1951) in chemistry from Spalding University in Louisville, Kentucky, and her Ph.D. degree (1961) in educational psychology from Indiana University.

Her entire academic career has been spent at Indiana University, where she has taught courses in measurement, statistics, psychology, and research methods in the School of Education. She served as research associate at the Institute of Educational Research and assistant director of the Bureau of Evaluative Studies and Testing for many years. Her publications include college textbooks in educational research and statistics and numerous monographs and articles on postsecondary education. She conducts workshops on classroom testing for faculty at Indiana University.

Clinton I. Chase graduated from the University of Idaho in 1950 with a B.S. degree in psychology and in 1951 also received an M.S. degree in administration there. After three-and-a-half years of service in the United States Air Force, he completed a Ph.D. degree (1958) in educational psychology with a specialty in measurement at the University of California, Berkeley. He then worked as a school psychologist in California. Since 1962, he has been a professor of educational psychology at Indiana University, where for eighteen years he was director of the Bureau of Evaluative Studies and Testing. He is a fellow in Division 15 (educational psychology) and Division 5 (measurement, statistics, and evaluation) of the American Psychological Association and has held offices in both the American Educational Research Association and the American Psychological Association. He is also the author of three other books and some seventy journal articles.

DEVELOPING AND USING TESTS EFFECTIVELY

1

Testing in the College Classroom

Tests are an integral part of most college courses. Thousands of tests are administered every day in college classrooms, and most of these tests are constructed by faculty members themselves. Mastery in writing classroom tests, however, is not a skill that all college teachers automatically possess. In fact, most college instructors feel poorly prepared to construct tests in their classes because they have never received any kind of formal training in this area. It is no wonder that many instructors view test construction and grading as one of the most difficult and unpleasant requirements of their courses. Furthermore, they have to fit test construction into a busy schedule that includes many other activities besides testing, such as preparing and delivering lectures, conducting research, and attending committee meetings. Consequently, many of the tests are hurriedly and often poorly constructed and are used in the wrong way. In discussing college teaching, Milton and Associates said, "Testing is perhaps the most neglected feature of good instruction" (1978, p. 101).

We submit that faculty members can learn to write good tests and that these tests can improve the quality of the teaching and learning process. Studies have consistently indicated that fairness in exams and grading is among the attributes that

1

contribute to effective teaching (Centra, 1981). Faculty need to remember that their tests are important to students because major decisions are going to be made by, and about, students on the basis of test scores and the resulting grade point average. So out of fairness to students, we must try to improve the tests we give. The goal of the following chapters is to help college instructors develop the skills needed for effective classroom testing.

Why are tests so important in college courses? We will put this question in the form of a multiple-choice item:

What is the purpose of classroom tests?

a. To arrive at grades for students
b. To assist instructors in planning content presentations
c. To facilitate and increase students' learning
d. To motivate students to study
e. All of the above

The best answer to the above question is (e), but many instructors use tests as though (a) were the correct answer. In fact, many of the problems associated with testing exist because instructors view tests as just a basis for grades. Too little emphasis has been placed on using tests to help teachers teach and students learn. Milton wrote that "a test is not only a grading device, but also a teaching technique in its own right" (1982, p. 31). When used properly, classroom tests not only measure educational achievement but also contribute to the effectiveness of both the teaching and the learning that go on in the classroom.

Tests Benefit Instructors

In the first place, the process of constructing tests itself is beneficial because it helps instructors put their courses in perspective. The writing of items forces instructors to think again about the really essential course objectives and content. They want their tests to emphasize the skills, knowledge, and abilities that they perceive to be most important in the course. If they want students to learn facts, they test them on their ability to recall information. But if they want to promote critical thinking, they write test items that emphasize understanding, application, and other higher-level skills. Their tests send a message to students: "Here are the really essential things to learn and remember from this course."

Tests also provide useful feedback about what students have and have not learned. To provide such information, tests can be used at three different times during a college course. Tests may be used at the beginning of a course (pretests) to see what skills students bring to a class. Faculty can measure students' knowledge of prerequisite material or concepts to be covered in the course and can plan their presentations accordingly. If students have not mastered the prerequisite knowledge and skills, instructors may have to spend some time teaching them; if they have already mastered some of the material to be taught in the course, instructors can spend time on other topics.

For example, a statistics instructor would use a pretest to measure students' proficiency in mathematics. If students have excellent mathematical skills, presentations of topics in statistics can be more direct and at a higher level than if students must be taught math skills along with statistical topics.

Pretests also provide a baseline for evaluating the changes over a semester's time and hence the effectiveness of the learning and instruction that have taken place. Foreign language instructors might find it useful to administer a pretest and a posttest (either the same test or an equivalent form) to measure the changes in students' proficiency over a semester. English composition instructors often give a writing test at the beginning and again at the end to see the changes in students' writing ability and hence to determine how much students have learned.

More commonly, tests are given during the course of a semester to assess the extent to which students are achieving the stated objectives. Classroom tests provide feedback on what students are learning in the class and thus help instructors to determine the effectiveness of their teaching of a particular segment (unit) of the course. By analyzing the test results, faculty can identify problem areas that perhaps should be reviewed or retaught before students move on to new material. Did they get

the main points from the reading assignments? Were they able
to apply a particular theory? Was some part of the material in
the unit more difficult for students than other parts? If most students have done poorly in some areas, the instructor does not
automatically assume that the students have not studied or that
they are not capable. There is a myth among some faculty
that the lower the test scores and the more students who fail,
the greater the indication that they are maintaining high standards and are offering an intellectually challenging course. But
instructors need to look at the instructional methods and procedures that they used. Maybe there is a better way to teach
the concepts, or perhaps more time should be set aside for the
instruction. Satisfactory performance on the part of the students,
by contrast, probably indicates that the teaching methods and
materials used have been effective.

The interrelationship among instruction, course objectives, and testing may be summarized as follows:

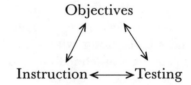

Instructors are generally aware of what they want students to
know or be able to do at the end of their course. It helps when
instructors state as explicit objectives what they want students
to achieve. These objectives can influence both instruction and
teaching. Through instruction, teachers present information
and materials designed to help students achieve the objectives.
The objectives also tell instructors what their tests should be
like, that is, what will be covered and with what emphasis. They
then write test items that measure achievement of the objectives.
The testing helps faculty determine the extent to which the objectives were achieved and hence the effectiveness of the instruction. Test results may then be the basis for changes in the method
of instruction or the course objectives.

Of course, classroom tests are an excellent way for teachers to motivate students to study the course material and thus to learn. It is a rare student who is not motivated to study for an announced test. Periodic tests will motivate students to review the content, seek solutions to unsolved problems, and synthesize material. Students' whole grasp of the subject matter will be strengthened by preparation for classroom tests. Although we would prefer that the motivation to learn were more intrinsic, we cannot ignore the extrinsic motivators. If tests are good ones that measure the attainment of important course objectives, then there is nothing wrong with using tests for motivation.

The tests given at the end of a course indicate the extent to which students have achieved the overall course objectives. These end-of-course tests, along with those given throughout the course, are generally used as a basis for arriving at students' grades. As we pointed out earlier, assigning grades is unfortunately often the main reason for testing.

Tests Benefit Students

The tests instructors give in class have an impact on both what and how students learn. Research and anecdotal evidence indicate that students learn according to how they are tested. Marton and Säljö (1976) wrote that students' approaches to learning could be classified into two broad categories: deep or surface approaches. Deep approaches involve a search for meaning, underlying principles, and links between different concepts or ideas. Surface approaches, by contrast, involve attempts to memorize course material, treating it as though the different facts and concepts were unrelated.

One important factor found to influence students' choice of a deep or surface learning approach is their perception of what will be demanded of them on subsequent examinations (Ramsden, 1985). If they believe instructors will emphasize factual recall in their tests, students will learn facts. If instructors are going to ask them to apply material to new situations, students will study and learn how to apply principles and theories. If students believe they will be required to analyze, synthesize, and make judgments, then they will learn to use higher-level thinking skills. E.M. Rogers, an award-winning physics teacher, described the effects of examinations on students as follows: "Examinations tell them our real aims, at least so they believe. If we stress clear understanding and aim at a growing knowledge of physics, we may completely sabotage our teaching by a final examination that asks for numbers to be put into memorized formulas. However loud our sermons, however intriguing the experiments, students will judge by that examination — and so will next year's students who hear about it" (1969, p. 956).

Some interesting observations on the relationship between exam content and learning were made in experiments with surrogate learners (Rigden and Tobias, 1991). The surrogate learners were faculty members and graduate students from fields other than science who tried to learn science in typical college classrooms. While theory was presented and discussed in class, none of it appeared on the exams, and students learned to treat the material as digressions. The professors were not happy with students' apparent indifference to the concepts. One of the surrogates explained: "While the professor was talking concepts, his exams were testing numerical solutions. And he probably never realized what the students knew very well, namely, that the *concepts* and the *history* didn't really count." (Rigden and Tobias, 1991, p. A52).

Tests thus provide a way for instructors to identify for students the facts, concepts, principles, and theories that are most important. Students look to the instructor who has the experience and knowledge in a subject area to identify for them what is important to learn and the content on which they can expect to be tested. Anderson said, "More than any other educational device, teacher-made tests tell students what the purpose of the instruction is and what is expected of them" (1987, p. 40). And as Walker observes, "The things that are *really* important, as every student knows, are the things that appear on tests and are used in grading" (1983, p. 173). As all instructors have probably observed, one of the most frequently asked questions on campus is, "Will that be on the test?" If we say yes, then the students actively make note and will certainly study that material. If we say no, students typically pay little or no further attention to that material. If we do not ask questions on the content of outside readings, for example, most students will not read the materials. There would be little point in preparing and distributing supplementary reading lists in this case.

A well-prepared test can provide a worthwhile learning experience in and of itself. J. B. Stroud, an early educational psychologist, once said, "It is probably not extravagant to say that the contribution made to a student's store of knowledge by the taking of an examination is as great, minute for minute, as any other enterprise he engages in" (1946, p. 476). Tests provide an opportunity for students to show what they have learned and to discover the scope and depth of their knowledge; they also tell students what they do not know and serve as a guide to further study. Students like to find out what they know, as do those of us who no longer take tests but who still enjoy tests of our knowledge. That may partially explain the popularity of the TV show "Jeopardy."

The best way to make a test a learning experience is to provide students with feedback, a confirmed essential of learning. They should be able to see how they have performed on each question on the test, to see what they got right as well as what was wrong. In this manner, students can see which topics they have managed, whether any problems exist, and whether their methods of study are effective. Feedback is most effective when it is given promptly. Unfortunately, too little feedback characterizes university teaching, especially in large classes. Often students are given only the total score, and this is not sufficient. Eble says, "Giving feedback on an examination is as necessary and as worthy of care, intelligence, and imagination as making up the test in the first place" (1988, p. 145).

If we accept the premise that the primary purpose of classroom testing is to facilitate students' learning, we will also want to give more frequent tests to provide the most feedback possible. A test at midsemester and one at the end are not sufficient to provide the feedback necessary for maximum learning in a course. In fact, students rarely receive any feedback from final examinations.

Basic Terminology

Before we discuss the development and proper use of tests in the college classroom, we need to introduce some of the basic terms that we will be using in these discussions in succeeding chapters.

Test

Typically a set of questions that students answer, a test is a systematic procedure for measuring students' achievement in the classroom. The questions, the administration, and the scoring are comparable for all students; hence the procedure is said to be systematic. Although tests do not always involve the familiar paper-and-pencil format, most of the ones discussed in this book are of that type. A test is necessarily a *sample* of behavior. Any test attempts to measure, at a particular point in time, a student's ability to show mastery of *some* information and *some* cognitive skills. Class time does not permit instructors to include on a single test all the questions that could be asked over the material. Rather, teachers must sample from the total content domain and infer from the sample how students might have performed on the entire body of material. It is thus very important that this sample of questions be representative. We want to get the same information from the test scores that we would get from any of the other possible samples we might choose. We will have more to say about this in a later chapter.

We sometimes call these samples of questions that we prepare tests, but other times we refer to them as examinations or quizzes. We generally distinguish between these terms based on the scope of the content covered and the importance (weight) assigned to the instrument in the final grade. Each involves the presentation of a standard set of questions to be answered, and each is intended to measure a sample of students' achievement of the coursework. An *examination* usually has a broader scope than a test. For example, we call the comprehensive instrument that we give at the end of a course or perhaps at midsemester an examination. It usually carries more weight in the overall grade composite. Some courses may have only one or two examinations. A *test* has a more limited scope, covering only a segment of the course content. There may be as many as three to four tests during the semester, each contributing to the final grade. A *quiz* is typically shorter, covering a much smaller segment of course material. Many professors like to give weekly quizzes just to ensure that students keep up with the reading and course assignments. Generally, a single quiz does not count as much in the final grade as a test or an exam, and students do not seem to get as anxious about a quiz.

While tests and examinations should always be scheduled so that students can prepare, quizzes are sometimes unannounced. We do not favor the unannounced, or "pop," quizzes, because we believe they may be somewhat unfair. Students should at least have the opportunity to approach classroom measurements on an even footing. For various reasons, students may not be able to be prepared every class meeting to take a quiz. The lucky ones who had time to read and study for that class will do well on the pop quiz; the others may do poorly. Because the results of such surprise quizzes will influence course grades, it seems fairer to students if all quizzes are announced.

The individual parts making up the test, exam, or quiz are called *items* or *questions*. We will use these terms interchangeably in this book.

Measurement and Evaluation

Following the administration of tests, examinations, or quizzes, instructors typically assign a numerical index to the students' performance that is called the score. The score usually represents the number of test items that a student answered correctly. This process of quantifying the students' performance is called *measurement*. *Evaluation* refers to the process of judging the value of the students' performance according to some standard and assigning an index that indicates quality. Evaluation is based on measurement but goes beyond it to answer the question of "how good." When we assign an A, B, or C to a test performance (score), we are giving an evaluation.

Norm-Referenced and Criterion-Referenced Tests

Achievement tests are classified as norm-referenced or criterion-referenced. The essential distinction between these two types is based on how the scores on the test are interpreted. On *norm-referenced tests,* instructors compare students' scores to one another and rank the students from best to poorest. Most tests given in the college classroom are norm-referenced, because instructors want to rank and spread students out to differentiate between them according to their achievement and to assign them a grade. For example, a norm-referenced test would permit us to say that student A was near the top of the group or scored higher than 95 percent of the group. We would not know exactly what the student knows, only that the student knows more than 95 percent of the class. If instructors want to make this kind of interpretation, the test should be designed for the purpose; that is, it would be designed to distribute students on a scale of achievement, from highest to lowest. The key feature in constructing norm-referenced tests is to select items that provide a wide range of scores. This is done by using items that are neither too easy nor too difficult but instead have an average level of difficulty.

On *criterion-referenced tests,* the scores are compared with some specified standard of acceptable performance. The performance of one student is interpreted with respect to mastery of content and other course objectives independently of the other students' performance. A typing test that finds a student can type sixty words per minute is criterion-referenced, because it states precisely what the student can do without any reference to the achievement of the other students in the class. On a criterion-referenced test, the students do not compete with one another but with a set of standards.

Criterion-referenced tests can be used in situations where there is a specified body of knowledge or skills that students must know. For example, a science instructor may give a test over terminology in a freshman science course or a test over bones and muscles in anatomy, on which the instructor specifies that students must get 85 percent of the questions correct to pass the test. The students who get at least 85 percent correct are called masters and are ready to move on to the next unit. The students who get fewer than 85 percent correct are nonmasters and must repeat the test until they reach the criterion. While the criterion is arbitrary, it is most often set at 85 percent correct. The criterion is set by determining the proficiency that students need to continue successfully to the next unit. Students who demonstrate the 85 percent level of proficiency generally have the background necessary to succeed on later material (Brown, 1981).

When constructing a criterion-referenced test, instructors are not concerned with obtaining a range of scores. They want to interpret the results to discover specific knowledge or skills that students demonstrate. Thus instructors are not concerned with how difficult the items are or how well the items discriminate between students. The items may be easy or difficult, depending on the nature of the subject matter. The key element is how well the items reflect the specific learning tasks. Typically, criterion-referenced tests sample a narrower range of content than a norm-referenced test does.

In summary, if the purpose of the test is to rank or differentiate between students, use a norm-referenced test; if the purpose is to ensure that students have mastered certain content and competencies, use a criterion-referenced test.

Speed Tests and Power Tests

A *speed test* is one with rigid time limits; it measures the number of items that an individual can complete in a given time. A *power test* generally has an ample time allowance and is designed to measure the maximum level of performance at which the student can perform. A pure power test has items arranged in order of increasing difficulty. In spite of the fact that classroom tests have to be completed within a specified time period, they are essentially power tests rather than speed tests, because the purpose is to find out what the students know, not how quickly they can tell us what they know. Instructors generally plan tests that can be completed in the time available for testing.

Objective and Subjective Tests

One of the most frequently asked student questions is, "Will the test be objective or subjective (essay)?" These terms have traditionally been used to refer to the response format of the questions on the test. *Objective tests* have questions with a choice format (multiple-choice, true-false, matching) or a completion format (fill-in-the-blank). *Subjective tests* require a constructed response.

Recent writers in the measurement field (Terwilliger, 1991) believe that the distinction based on response format is confusing and should be eliminated. Terwilliger stresses that objectivity in tests is based on more than response format. If there is high degree of consensus among experts judging the correctness of a response to a question, the test is objective. If there is little consensus among experts concerning the correctness of a response, the test is subjective. Objectivity is not guaranteed simply because an item has a blank to complete or a choice format that permits scoring by machine or a clerical worker. It is possible that some essay questions could be more objective than some poorly written multiple-choice or true-false questions. Through the use of model answers, scoring keys, and trained readers, essay tests can be scored with a great deal of objectivity. Some multiple-choice or completion questions, on the other hand, could fail to elicit responses on which subject matter experts agree. Hence, Terwilliger argues that they should not be labeled objective questions. In conclusion, objectivity should not be considered an "all or nothing" concept; there are degrees of objectivity in tests. Objectivity is a goal that instructors should strive for in all types of measurement.

Gronlund (1990) suggested that we substitute the terms *selection* and *supply* for *objective* and *subjective* to refer to test response formats. Terwilliger uses the terms *choice response* and *free response* to describe the formats. In spite of the potential confusion, we may occasionally use the terms objective and subjective in the traditional way in this book. As used to distinguish between test formats, these terms are firmly entrenched in the measurement lexicon, and college faculty and students will undoubtedly continue to use them.

Formative and Summative Tests

Formative tests are given several times during the course of a semester and generally cover a predefined segment of a course. Formative tests provide ongoing feedback to teachers and students about how learning is proceeding. Instructors use formative tests for modifying instructional methods and materials, and students use them for directing advanced or remedial study.

Summative tests are given at the conclusion of a course and are used mainly to determine the extent to which students have achieved the objectives of the course. They represent a final report about the effectiveness of the teachers' instruction and of the students' learning of the course content. Summative tests are principally used for grading.

Problems with College Tests

The following is a listing of some of the problems with college tests that keep them from contributing as much as they should to improved teaching and learning.

1. Tests do not focus on what is most important. They include too many questions requiring only knowledge of facts and trivia and provide no intellectual challenge to the students. Students often complain that test content does not reflect the material discussed in class or what the professor seemed to indicate was most important. They often feel somewhat cheated when they have put forth a great deal of effort and then take a test that does not permit them to show what they have learned.

2. Too little feedback is provided. In too many instances, students learn only their total score and never get to see what answers they got wrong. Research and common sense tell us that it is difficult to improve unless one knows how one is currently doing. One cannot become a better sharpshooter without knowing how close to the target the previous shots have come. Similarly, if students are to improve, they must be provided with information about which answers were correct and which were incorrect. Also, students complain that professors take too long to return tests to them. Feedback is most effective when it is given promptly

3. The questions are often ambiguous and unclear. Milton and Associates (1978) said that ambiguous questions constitute the major weakness in college tests. Ambiguous questions often appear on tests, either because instructors fear that very direct questions will give away the answer and make the test too easy or because instructors are in a hurry and put off writing tests until the last minute. Editing and an independent review of the test items by a colleague can help to minimize this problem.

4. The tests are too short to sample adequately the body of content that was covered. Tests that are too short introduce undue error into our measurement and are not fair to students.

5. Instructors fail to communicate to students the purpose of their classroom tests and how the results will aid learning. An adversarial relationship often develops between instructors and students. Students feel that teachers are out to get them and are using exams for that purpose. A colleague at another institution told us about a student's reaction when she returned quiz papers on which most students had done poorly. The student came up to her after class and said, "I suppose you are going home to celebrate." When she asked, "Celebrate what?" the student said, "Well, because you really got us on that quiz." This instructor was quite taken aback by the student's assumption that poor test scores were a cause for celebration on the instructor's part.

6. Many college courses do not have enough exams to provide a good sample of students' attainment of the knowledge and skills the courses are trying to develop. The more samples of student achievement teachers obtain, the more feedback students receive and the more confidence faculty can have in the accuracy of their course grades. A related problem is that many instructors wait too long to give the first exam. Students need to know how they are doing in the course before midsemester.

In the following chapters, we will discuss ways to eliminate such problems and improve the tests given in the college classroom.

Overview

The challenge to college faculty is to develop tests that measure significant learning and measure it accurately. Developing tests that measure students' achievement well entails several steps: planning, construction, administration, and evaluation. In the planning stage, instructors must think about the content to be covered on the test, the cognitive skills to be assessed, and the kinds of questions to be used. Having made these decisions, instructors are ready to write the test questions. Guidelines for writing different types of test questions will be presented in the following chapters. After test items have been prepared, careful attention should be given to assembling the items, writing directions, and administering the test. Lack of attention to such factors may adversely affect the test results. Once the test has been administered, teachers should evaluate it by looking at the item response pattern to determine how difficult and discriminating the items were.

We will discuss these steps in the following chapters.

Summary

Classroom tests and examinations are extremely important educational tools that contribute to both the teaching and the learning process. They define what is important in the course, motivate students to study, and provide feedback to instructors and students. Unfortunately, not all college teachers know how to write good tests, and this chapter has discussed some of the problems frequently found in college tests. Test construction is a skill that can be learned, however, and the purpose of this book is to help college instructors develop it.

2

Planning the Test

Good classroom tests require planning. Faculty cannot effectively measure students' learning with a test they have hurriedly put together at the last minute. Before any items are written, instructors need to develop a test plan that specifies clearly what they are going to measure on the test. A test plan enables the instructor to create an instrument that *tests* what has been *taught*. At this stage, faculty must also decide on the response format, length, and difficulty level of the test. In this chapter, we first look at the procedure for developing the test plan and then focus on the guidelines for making other relevant decisions.

A test plan typically has two components: the content to be covered and the cognitive skills to be measured on the test. Most instructors have other course objectives like the students' development of new interests, appreciations, and attitudes, but they do not try to measure such affective objectives in classroom tests. In this chapter, we are concerned only with the testing of cognitive objectives.

The content dimension of the test plan is straightforward. The course syllabus or the table of contents in the text usually provides the framework for the material covered. In the test plan, the instructor lists the content categories to be tested. Some subtopics may be listed under each major content category. Instructors want to make sure, however, that they include only content that was taught òr assigned for learning. Including other content would be unfair to students, who are justifiably concerned about fairness in classroom tests.

In the second part of the plan, the instructor is concerned with the measurement of cognitive skills — the intellectual processes that students use to construct answers to the test questions. Faculty should be concerned not only with what students have learned but also with how they can use the knowledge. Do instructors want their students to simply recall information, or do they want them to analyze, synthesize, apply, and evaluate? Instructors need to recall the cognitive skills emphasized during the instruction, the kinds of questions asked in class, the nature of the assignments, and so on, and make sure that they require these same skills on the test.

Cognitive Objectives

There are various ways that faculty can categorize the cognitive skills to be measured on classroom tests. One of the most useful classifications is that provided by Bloom (1956). This classification identifies six cognitive skills whose attainment instructors should promote in the college classroom and measure on their tests. Bloom's system arranges cognitive skills in a hierarchy from simple to complex. Each higher-level skill utilizes the lower-level ones and demands greater intellect from the learner. Knowledge is the least demanding but serves as the basis for the higher-level cognitive skills. Students have to comprehend material before they can apply or analyze it. Evaluation is the most demanding of the cognitive skills because it requires judgments using criteria recalled by the learner. The skills, in the order of complexity or intellectual demand, are knowledge, comprehension, application, analysis, synthesis, and evaluation. Figure 2.1 shows the hierarchical arrangement of Bloom's cognitive skills.

Figure 2.1. Bloom's Cognitive Objectives
Arranged from Simple to Complex.

We now consider these categories in more detail:

1. *Knowledge* refers to the recall of previously learned material. Students are required to remember facts, principles,
   steps in a sequence, and other information in the same way
   in which the material was presented in class. The key activity is *recall*. Example: Identify the "wage fund doctrine."
2. *Comprehension* refers to the understanding of learned material. Students must show that they grasp the meaning of
   the material by explaining, interpreting, translating to a
   new form or symbol system, and extrapolating. The key
   activity is *explain*. Example: Explain the statement: Aquinas
   was to Aristotle what Marx was to Ricardo.
3. *Application* refers to the ability to use learned material in
   new and concrete situations. Students must use abstractions,
   such as concepts, principles, rules, theories, and laws, to
   find solutions to new problems. The key activity is *transfer*.
   Example: Use the "wage fund doctrine" to explain wage rate
   in the writing of J. S. Mill.
4. *Analysis* refers to the ability to break down material into its
   component parts so that the organizational structure is understood. Students are required to determine distinguish-
   ing characteristics, show the relationship between parts, and
   so on. The key activity is *separate*. Example: Compare and
   contrast the attitudes toward male and female sex roles in
   the work of Ibsen and Huysmans.
5. *Synthesis* refers to the ability to put parts together to form
   a new whole that was not previously present. Students must
   think creatively to produce new products, such as a theme,
   speech, article, or research proposal. The key activity is

combine. Example: Compose an essay discussing how Nietzsche and Marx's approach to the question of "truth" differed from that of a positivist such as Comte.

6. *Evaluation* refers to the ability to judge the value of material for a given purpose using definite criteria. Students are required to make value judgments, to rate ideas or objects, and to accept or reject materials based on standards. The key activity is *make judgment.* Example: Using the five criteria discussed in class, critically evaluate Adam Smith's theory of economic development.

**Table 2.1. Examples of Student Activities and
Verbs for Bloom's Cognitive Levels.**

Bloom's Cognitive Level	Student Activity	Words to Use in Item Stems
Knowledge	Remembering facts, terms, concepts, definitions, principles	Define, list, state, identify, label, name, who? when? where? what?
Comprehension	Explaining/interpreting the meaning of material	Explain, predict, interpret, infer, summarize, convert, translate, give example, account for, paraphrase
Application	Using a concept or principle to solve a problem	Apply, solve, show, make use of, modify, demonstrate, compute
Analysis	Breaking material down into its component parts to see interrelationships/ hierarchy of ideas	Differentiate, compare/ contrast, distinguish ___ from ___, how does ___ relate to ___ ? why does ___ work?
Synthesis	Producing something new or original from component parts	Design, construct, develop, formulate, imagine, create, change, write a poem or short story
Evaluation	Making a judgment based on a preestablished set of criteria	Appraise, evaluate, justify, judge, which would be better?

Source: Adapted from Goodwin and others, n.d.

We sometimes refer to knowledge, comprehension, and application as lower-level cognitive skills and analysis, synthesis, and evaluation as higher-level cognitive skills. Table 2.1 shows an outline of Bloom's cognitive objectives and some of the words that might be used in test items to elicit the various cognitive skills.

Exhibit 2.1 shows multiple-choice items intended to measure cognitive skills at the various levels of Bloom's taxonomy. The classification of test questions into specific categories is, however, somewhat arbitrary. One person may believe that an item measures application, while another thinks that it measures analysis. That is the reason some writers merge the skills into just two categories: lower-level and higher-level cognitive skills. The goal is to write test items that measure a variety of skills, especially at the higher levels. Instructors may sometimes have to use their best judgment about what higher intellectual skills their questions measure, but certainly they should recognize those that measure only factual knowledge. Faculty can ask a colleague who is familiar with the course content to read their questions and try to classify them at the various levels of Bloom's taxonomy. Additionally, if instructors want to measure at higher levels like application or analysis, they must use novel situations in the questions. If they use the same example or situation that was used in class or in the text, then the question may be measuring only recall of that information and not application or analysis at all.

Exhibit 2.2 provides another illustration of Bloom's taxonomy. Taking a single concept — test reliability — we have written a test item about that concept at each of the cognitive levels.

Table of Specifications

A good classroom test should sample the course content and measure the cognitive skills emphasized in the unit being tested. The easiest way to ensure a representative sample is to prepare a table of specifications. A *table of specifications* is a two-way chart with the content topics on one dimension and cognitive skills on the other. The chart relates the cognitive skills to the course content and indicates the relative emphasis to be given to each

Exhibit 2.1. Multiple-Choice Items That Measure at Various Levels.

---

1. Knowledge
   Which of the following are the raw materials for photosynthesis?
   a. Water, heat, sunlight
   b. Carbon dioxide, sunlight, oxygen
   c. Water, carbon dioxide, sunlight
   d. Sunlight, oxygen, carbohydrates
   e. Water, carbon dioxide, carbohydrates
2. Comprehension
   If living cells similar to those found on earth were found on another planet
   where there was no molecular oxygen, which cell part would most likely be
   absent?
   a. Cell membrane
   b. Nucleus
   c. Mitochondria
   d. Ribosome
   e. Chromosomes
3. Application
   Phenylketonuria (PKU) is an autosomal recessive condition. About one in
   every fifty individuals is heterozygous for the gene but shows no symptoms of
   the disorder. If you select a symptom-free male and a symptom-free female at
   random, what is the probability that they could have a child afflicted with PKU?
   a. $(.02)(.02)(.25) = 0.0001 = 0.01\%$, or about $1/10,000$
   b. $(.02)(.02) = 0.0004 = 0.04\%$, or about $1/2,500$
   c. $(1)(50)(2) = 100\% = $ all
   d. $(1)(50)(0) = 0 = $ none
   e. $1/50 = 2\%$, or $2/100$
4. Analysis
   Mitochondria are called the powerhouses of the cell because they make energy
   available for cellular metabolism. Which of the following observations is *most*
   cogent in supporting this concept of mitochondrial function?
   a. ATP occurs in the mitochondria.
   b. Mitochondria have a double membrane.
   c. The enzymes of the Krebs cycle, and molecules required for terminal
      respiration, are found in mitochondria.
   d. Mitochondria are found in almost all kinds of plant and animal cells.
   e. Mitochondria abound in muscle tissue.
5. Evaluation
   Disregarding the relative feasibility of the following procedures, which of these
   lines of research is likely to provide us with the most valid and direct evidence
   as to evolutionary relations among different species?
   a. Analysis of the chemistry of stored food in female gametes
   b. Analysis of the enzymes of the Krebs cycle
   c. Observations of the form and arrangement of the endoplasmic reticulum
   d. Comparison of details of the molecular structure of DNA
   e. Determination of the total percent protein in the cells

Note: The writers are indebted to Dr. Michael Tansey of the biology department of Indiana University, Bloomington, for these items.

Exhibit 2.2. Single Concept Measured at Different Levels.

---

1. Knowledge
   The split-half technique is used to establish a test's
   a. Reliability   c. Objectivity
   b. Validity   d. Correlation with a criterion
2. Comprehension
   If a test is doubled in length by adding comparable items, the reliability
   coefficient
   a. Remains the same   c. Will increase by some amount
   b. Will be doubled   d. May or may not increase
3. Application
   An odd-even correlation coefficient of .80 is obtained for a 100-item test.
   What is the estimated reliability of the entire test?
   a. .64   b. .78   c. .89   d. .91
4. Analysis
   Which of the following steps would most likely lead to an increase in the
   reliability estimate for a test?
   a. Increasing the number of persons tested from 500 to 1,000
   b. Selecting items so that half were very difficult and half very easy
   c. Increasing the length of the test with more of the same kinds of items
   d. Increasing the homogeneity of the group of subjects tested
5. Synthesis
   An instructor plans to use the split-half method to obtain an estimate of the
   reliability of a 100-item speed test covering math computation. Explain to
   this instructor why the split-half method should *not* be used; recommend
   an alternative procedure and defend your choice.
6. Evaluation
   An instructor in an introductory psychology course administered a 150-item
   multiple-choice comprehensive final exam in a course. The items had a range
   of difficulty from easy to hard. Which of the following would be the *best* procedure for determining the reliability of the test?
   a. The coefficient of equivalence
   b. The coefficient of stability
   c. Kuder-Richardson formula 21
   d. Split-half

---

type of learning outcome. Table 2.2 shows a hypothetical table of specifications for a test that will measure knowledge, comprehension, and application of five content topics. No one classroom test has to measure all six of the cognitive skills, but certainly a good test measures more than knowledge.

The numbers at the bottom of each column in Table 2.2 indicate the percentage of the test devoted to a particular cognitive skill. In this hypothetical test, 30 percent of the test items will measure knowledge, 50 percent comprehension, and 20

Table 2.2. Hypothetical Table of Specifications.

| Content | Skills | | | Total |
	Knowledge	Comprehension	Application	(%)
A	6	10	4	20
B	3	5	2	10
C	3	5	2	10
D	9	15	6	30
E	9	15	6	30
Total (%)	30	50	20	100

percent application. The distribution according to content areas can be seen in the last column of the table; hence, 20 percent of the test will cover Topic A, 10 percent Topic C, and so on. The classroom instructor decides the relative emphasis to be placed on the various content areas and cognitive objectives. Using the percentages assigned to each content and skill category, the instructor determines the weight to be given each cell in the table. For example, since 20 percent of the test is to cover content Topic A, 30 percent is to cover Topic D, and 50 percent is to measure comprehension, 10 percent ($.50 \times .20$) of the items will measure comprehension of Topic A, and 15 percent ($.50 \times .30$) will measure comprehension of Topic D. The instructor then easily determines the *number* of items to write for each cell of the table by taking the appropriate percentage of the total number planned for the test. For example, if the hypothetical test is to have a total of forty items, then six ($.15 \times 40$) items will be written to cover comprehension of Topic D and four to cover comprehension of Topic A.

The process of developing a table of specifications can greatly improve instructor-made tests. The table indicates the content to cover and the number and kinds of questions to write so that instructors are able to develop a test that reflects what they have taught. A table of specifications helps professors avoid one of the most common problems in classroom tests, namely writing all items at the knowledge level. These items are the easiest to write, so unless instructors have a guide to follow they are likely to end up with too many low-level questions. A test plan not only guides the instructor in writing the test but also informs students about what they can expect to find on the test. The table of specifications is discussed more thoroughly in Chapter Three, where we make a specific application of it.

When specifying the content for a classroom test, instructors must also decide whether they will give unit tests covering only the material since the last test or cumulative tests that go back to material previously tested. Either is acceptable for formative tests. Students, of course, typically prefer unit tests because there is less material to learn. The nature of the course content may determine whether cumulative tests are used. In hierarchical courses like math, statistics, and foreign languages, the students have to keep using previously learned content, so questions over earlier material could be included on each test. Having cumulative tests is undoubtedly an advantage for students who must take comprehensive final exams (Dempster, 1987). We do recommend that final exams be comprehensive because studying for them gives students a chance to integrate material and see the total picture. The review of the material required on a comprehensive test also promotes students' long-term retention. Comprehensive finals also permit instructors to write test items that cross content topics.

Other Decisions to Be Made at the Planning Stage

Before instructors start to write the test, they must decide on the format and length of the test and the difficulty of the test items.

The Test Format

After planning what content and cognitive skills to measure, instructors must decide on the best way to do it; that is, they must decide on the test format. The format refers to whether the test will have recognition-type items (multiple-choice, true-false, matching) or essay items. Sometimes the cognitive skill(s) to be measured on the test will determine the format for them. If instructors want students to take a position on an issue and defend it, then they would most likely use an essay format. But many times faculty have a choice. Many cognitive abilities formerly believed to be amenable only to essay questions can be tested with multiple-choice or recognition items. A common stereotype depicts multiple-choice tests as measuring simple factual recall and essays as evaluating higher-order thinking. However, a study by Bennett, Rock, and Wang (1991) finds little support for this stereotype. Multiple-choice items can be written to measure reasoning, comprehension, application, and other complex thinking processes. There sometimes are other reasons, however, for choosing one format over the other.

The characteristics and relative advantages and disadvantages of the two formats are summarized as follows:

Free Response	*Choice*
1. Requires student to organize and express answer in own words.	Requires student to select the correct answer from among several options.
2. Consists of fewer questions, each calling for more lengthy answer.	Has more questions, but each takes less time to answer.
3. Limits sampling of content.	Broadens coverage of content.
4. Is relatively easy to prepare, but difficult to score.	Is difficult to construct, but easy to score.
5. Is susceptible to bluffing.	Is susceptible to guessing.
6. Scoring is more subjective.	Scoring is more objective and reliable.

What factors do faculty consider when deciding on the format for the test?

What Is to Be Measured. For some learning outcomes, the recognition item is the most efficient; for others, the essay item is most satisfactory. The best advice to faculty is to use the format that seems more appropriate for measuring the outcomes of interest. To measure students' ability to develop an argument or a research plan, faculty would probably use essay items. If a course objective in a journalism class, for example, is that students are able to explain the role of the press in the coming of the Civil War, the instructor might find the essay item to be the most suitable type for measuring this objective. To measure the extent of pupils' factual knowledge, comprehension, or ability to analyze or to apply principles, faculty could use a recognition-type item such as multiple-choice. If a course objective is that students are able to identify the authors of selected writings about the coming of the Civil War, the instructor might find a recognition-type item to be more appropriate.

The Size of the Class. When deciding what types of tests to use, class size is often the most important factor to consider. If instructors are teaching very large lecture classes (introductory level), it is difficult to give essay or even short-answer or completion tests. The time required to score them would be prohibitive. Instructors in large classes typically choose the recognition-type test that permits machine scoring.

Cross (1990) surveyed 1,100 randomly selected professors from small, medium, and large colleges and universities across the nation about the types of tests they use and their beliefs about the best method(s) for assessing students' learning. He finds that class size is the factor that professors consider most important when they decide what types of tests to use in their classes. They use multiple-choice tests most often in large classes. In their small classes (mean size = 16), they use essay tests most often. Over two-thirds say that size of class prevents them from using their preferred type of test. As expected, they tend to use the test type they prefer in their small classes, but not in their large ones.

Time Available to Prepare and Score Test. It takes a long time to prepare a multiple-choice test. By contrast, it takes a long time to score essay tests. So the instructor must consider whether more time will be available when preparing or when scoring the test. If instructors are short of time when a test must be prepared, then they might choose an essay test, if class size permits. Ease of construction of essay items may be more apparent than real, however; they are easier only because fewer questions have to be written. Limited time to prepare a test is not a good reason to choose the essay format. Faculty should use the essay format because they feel it is the best format for measuring the content and objectives, not because they have not allotted sufficient time to prepare a number of multiple-choice items.

Of course, the instructor can use both formats on the same test. Many instructors who use mainly multiple-choice items like to have at least one essay question on the test. Having the two formats enables faculty to capitalize on the strengths of both. An essay question provides a sample of students' ability to reason and to present their ideas in coherent prose. Having an essay question may also have a positive influence on the way students study for tests. Some research shows that students study more thoroughly for essay-type exams than for recognition tests (D'Ydewalle, Swerts, and deCorte, 1983).

Instructors can also vary the format from time to time during the semester. Research shows that students differ in their preference for different types of exams, so using a variety of test formats would give students an opportunity to do their best work. Bracht (1967) surveyed college students and found that 61 percent prefer the test format to be part objective and part essay. Twenty-six percent prefer objective tests exclusively, and only 13 percent prefer essay exams exclusively. Bracht found a high correlation between test format preference and the format on which students perceive their performance is better. In another study, a majority (59 percent) of over 5,000 freshmen surveyed at Indiana University in 1991 said they prefer to take multiple-choice tests; only 18 percent prefer essays. When asked the kind of test they *least* prefer, 52 percent said long essay, and 32 percent said true-false questions (*A Freshman Profile,* 1991).

Once instructors decide to use choice items, essay, or both, the next step is to select the particular type of recognition or essay item that they want to use. The advantages and limitations of each type, along with guidelines for making this decision, are discussed in Chapters Four, Five, and Six.

Test Length

The length of the test is often influenced by the time available to an instructor for administering it. Most formative tests are administered during fifty-minute class periods, so instructors choose the number of items that students can complete in that time. Instructors can use a greater number of items and item types on summative (final) examinations, when students may have as long as two hours for the exam.

The type and difficulty of the items used will also influence the number that can be included on the test. Essay items require more time to answer, so fewer can be used. The time required to answer an essay question depends on the nature of the question and how much discussion the instructor wants. Allow about ten to fifteen minutes for a short essay and thirty minutes for the extended essay requiring two to three pages.

Completion items require more time than true-false, and the latter require less time than multiple-choice. As a rule of thumb, instructors should allow about one minute per item for multiple-choice or completion items and about one-half minute for each true-false. A short-answer question requiring a sentence or two requires about two minutes to answer. Multiple-choice items measuring higher-level thinking may take a little more time, depending on the complexity of the question and the length of the options. In a fifty-minute period, the instructor can thus plan on using about forty to forty-five multiple-choice items or about sixty or so true-false items (these are all just suggested times). The remaining class time is needed to distribute and collect test booklets, give any necessary directions, answer questions, and so on.

Instructors may have to determine, through experience, the time limits that are realistic for their students and their particular test questions. Instructors can count on the rule of thumb that the fastest student will typically finish a test in about half the time required by the slowest student. Remember that students should have time at least to attempt all of the items.

Of course, instructors must keep in mind that the longer the test, the more reliable it tends to be. We generally recommend including as many items as students can answer in the time available.

What about optional items on a test? Many professors who use essay exams like to give students a choice of questions to answer. Students like to have a choice, too, because optional questions provide a better opportunity to show what they know and create less anxiety about the test. Permitting students to choose which of several test questions to answer, however, is not considered sound measurement practice. When instructors give students a choice between questions, they are actually administering several different tests and thus are not evaluating all students on the same basis. For example, if there are five essay questions on a test and the instructions are to answer any three of them, then ten different tests could result. (Aiken, 1989, reports that if there are m items and the instructions are to answer any s of them, there are $m!/s! \, (m-s)!$ possible tests. If $m = 5$ and $s = 3$, then there are $(5 \cdot 4 \cdot 3 \cdot 2 \cdot 1)/(3 \cdot 2 \cdot 1)(2 \cdot 1)$ or 10 different tests.)

The items on these different tests may not be equally difficult, so some students could get higher scores, not necessarily because they knew more but because they selected easier items. Other students could be penalized because they were challenged by the more difficult items. Also, when students know they are going to have a choice between items, they sometimes do not study all the material thoroughly. If instructors believe that all the course material is important and that all students should master it, then they should require students to answer all the questions. Instructors are not being unfair to students when they do not give them a choice between the questions. Similarly, we do not recommend that instructors include extra-credit questions on a test. If students are going to be compared for grading purposes, they should all take the same test.

Item Difficulty

If a test is being used to discriminate between students to assign grades, then instructors should prepare a test that will produce a spread of scores. On an objective test, items of average difficulty — those items answered correctly by 50 percent of the students — provide the widest distribution of scores. As a rule of thumb, we recommend using items that 50 to 70 percent of the students can answer correctly. An item should be difficult enough that students who have not studied will get it wrong but easy enough that students who have studied will get it right. Items that are very easy or very hard produce a narrower range of scores and therefore discriminate less between various levels of achievement. It is satisfactory to begin a test with an easy item or two for motivational purposes. We may also have a few difficult items to challenge the brighter students. But the majority of the items should be of average difficulty.

If instructors are using the item for the very first time, they may have to rely on their own judgment about the item's difficulty. Of course, after an objective item has been used, an analysis of the results will indicate the percentage of students who answered it correctly.

It is not always easy, however, to interpret item difficulty. An item may be difficult because of the way it is constructed (it may be ambiguous), because the concept being measured is complex, because it calls for higher-level thinking, or because the students failed to study the material. When instructors are trying to interpret item difficulty indices, they should look at the construction of the item and the content and cognitive skill being measured as well as the students' learning experiences.

Frequency of Tests

There are no rules about testing frequency; the number of tests should be determined by the difficulty and amount of material covered and by the level of the class. But we recommend more than just a midterm and a final during a semester. Having too few tests deprives students and instructor of feedback on their progress and contributes to a lack of student motivation. By contrast, too many tests impinge on class time needed for instruction and teacher time needed for preparing class instruction, spent, instead, on preparing and grading tests. In most semester courses, two to three tests plus the final examination seem a reasonable number. Crooks (1988) reports on a meta-analysis that reviews research on the effects of test frequency on final examination performance. A gain in final exam performance is found to be associated with a moderate frequency of testing. Groups that receive no testing during the course are at a definite disadvantage on the final exam. The studies that measure student attitudes toward instruction show that students favor more frequent testing. Having several test grades also provides a more reliable basis for assigning a course grade.

Instructors should not wait too long to give the first test in a course. It should probably be given after the third or fourth week of the semester. An early test gets students started studying rather than waiting until a midsemester exam. It also gives students some idea of the kind of learning that instructors expect; any problems can be identified early while there is still time to remediate them. Waiting until midsemester to have the first test promotes bad study habits, denies students early feedback, and gives them a false impression of what college is like. Some students are hopelessly behind by the time the first test is given.

Summary

The quality of classroom tests depends to a great extent on the care and effort spent by the instructor in the planning stage. A test plan requires instructors to specify the content topics and cognitive skills they want to measure on the test. Bloom's taxonomy, which includes the cognitive skills of knowledge, comprehension, application, analysis, synthesis, and evaluation, provides a useful way to classify faculty objectives in the college classroom. A table of specifications guides the writing of test questions by indicating the number and types of items needed to create a representative sample of course content and cognitive skills. With good planning, the test will directly reflect what instructors have been teaching their students.

Guidelines were also given in this chapter for making decisions about test length and format and difficulty of the test items. Instructors should include as many items as students can answer in the time available; longer tests are usually more dependable as indicators of students' learning than short tests.

3

Reliability
and Validity

This chapter deals with two of the most important concepts in measurement, reliability and validity. No matter what we are measuring — the distance to a planet, the width of a room, the height of a mountain, the amount of anxiety one feels — the reliability and validity questions loom large. *Reliability* deals with the consistency of measurements; *validity* deals with appropriateness of information for making decisions. If any measurement is to be useful, we have to have confidence that the data, if replicated, would produce the same values and that the values are relevant for making a conclusion about a characteristic of an object or individual we are attempting to assess. In the following pages, we elaborate on these concepts, show how they are applied in classroom testing, and illustrate their interpretation.

Reliability

An old carpenters' adage illustrates the concept of reliability quite well. It says, "measure twice, and saw once!" To be sure we have indeed measured with consistency, a second measurement is needed to verify the first. If the measurements agree, we have measured consistently, that is, reliably. If I were going to put a carpet in my office, I would ask my graduate assistant to measure

32

the length and width of the room. If the assistant measures the dimensions twice, would the second measurement be the same as the first? The same question arises in regard to measuring any mental function, such as achievement of instructional objectives. If an instructor builds a test of achievement of instructional objectives, and if the instructor measures students a second time, will the two testings rank each student about the same? If so, the test is reliable; that is, the test has placed the students in about the correct position among their classmates. Substantial reliability in all tests is a goal that says tests are measuring in a consistent, not haphazard, manner.

Ways to Determine Test Reliability

Since reliability deals with consistency of measurement, anyone assessing the reliability of a test has to have at least two measurements of a trait for a common group of people. The test maker will then compare these measurements to see if the position of individuals on one is consistent with their position on the other. In all techniques for assessing the reliability of a test, faculty must have, for each student, at least two measurements of the trait being assessed. Psychometric specialists have devised several ways for doing this. Faculty could use two "parallel," or equivalent forms, but instructors do not always have two forms of a test. Instructors could use the same test with a time lapse between the two administrations, but this test-retest procedure is not very satisfactory because students remember the test items, talk to one another, and consult their books and notes. The second test would be on a different playing field.

A very useful procedure is to make two tests from a single test by splitting it into two halves. We get one score on the odd-numbered items and a second score on the even-numbered items. Or we can look at how consistently students perform from item to item on one test, in effect treating every item as a separate very small test and hence comparing scores across many minitests.

For classroom testing, only two of these procedures are very practical to apply — the splitting of a test into two parts, resulting in two half-test scores, and the comparing of student responses for consistency across all items. These two techniques are referred to as the *split-half* and the *internal consistency* procedures, respectively. Here is a look at these procedures in more detail.

Split-Half Procedure. Before a test maker can draw a conclusion about the consistency of tests, there must be on hand two measurements of each of the students on a single area of expertise. One very common way to get these two measurements is to treat one half of a test as one measurement and the other half as a second measurement. If all items in the test are focused on a common domain of knowledge, then the test user may think of each half of the test as an appropriate sample of that domain. It therefore seems reasonable to compare students' scores on one half of the test with their scores on the other half to see how consistently they measure.

There is, however, a problem with this comparison; short tests are less reliable than long ones. By cutting the test in half, we have made two short tests, neither of which is as reliable as the long test from which it was created. For example, if we went to the reservoir and took four samples of water and tested each sample's bacterial content, our conclusion about the purity of the water would be less reliable than if we had tested eight samples. A similar idea applies to tests. If we sample a skill with a longer set of test items, the test will be more reliable than if we use a shorter set of items.

How shall faculty deal, then, with the half test as a measure of the skill they want to assess? Luckily, there is a procedure for managing this problem. When a test is split in two, the reliability estimate between the two short tests will be lower than the reliability expected from the full-length test. To estimate the reliability of a test of the original length, we apply the Spearman-Brown prophecy formula.

We obtain a measure of a test's reliability by using a procedure called *correlation* to compare students' scores on one half of a test with their scores on the other half. Users of this book probably do not need to calculate correlation coefficients, but they will no doubt see correlations and will want to know what the values mean.

Correlation coefficients tell us how well one set of scores from a group of individuals corresponds with a second set; that is, does a person's position in the group as shown by the first set of data match that person's position as shown by the second set of data? Correlation coefficients are expressed in values from 0 to 1.0 and from 0 to − 1.0. *Negative correlations* appear when the students who score high on the first test score low on the second test, while those who score low on the first test score high on the second test. The positive values indicate that students' rank on one test tends to be matched by their rank on the other test. The closer this match for all students, the closer the correlation is to 1.00. With a positive correlation between two half-test scores, a student who does well on one half of the test is projected, with some confidence, to have a good score on the other half, while a student with a low score on the first test would be projected to get a low score on the second test.

If the correlation is near zero, a test user's confidence in projecting one score from another is nil; that is, knowledge of a score on one half of the test will provide no basis for projecting what the score will be on the other half.

However, the accuracy of prediction is not a straight line relationship between the two measurements. As coefficients get larger, that is, nearer 1.0, the degree of accuracy of predicting one set of scores from another gets disproportionately larger. For example, below a correlation coefficient of .50, prediction of one measurement from another begins to be uncertain, but confidence in a correlation coefficient of, say, .75 is about twice that of .50. With a value of .90, an instructor's confidence that one set of scores for a group will accurately reflect a second set of parallel scores for that same group increases to over three times what it would be at .50.

Because the correspondence of two sets of scores on a common measure goes up more and more rapidly as we move farther above .50, faculty should look for values well above .50 when looking at reliability coefficients for their tests. Indeed, test users should hope to find them above .70 and would like to find them in the .80 range. Correlations in this range tell instructors that the students came reasonably close to matching their scores on one half of the test with their scores on the other half.

The typical procedure for splitting a test into two halves is to get one score from the odd-numbered test items and the other from the even-numbered ones. This method provides two measurements for each student on the same domain. These measurements are then correlated to produce a coefficient. However, as we noted earlier, the half test will not be as reliable as the full-length test. To project this half-test correlation into the value for the full test, instructors apply the Spearman-Brown formula:

$$r = \frac{2 \times \text{the correlation between the two half scores}}{1 + \text{the correlation between the two half scores}},$$

where r is the reliability of the test when the two halves are put back together into a single test.

Many test analysis programs used by colleges across the country will report the Spearman-Brown reliability.

Internal Consistency Methods. Like the Spearman-Brown procedure, methods developed by Kuder and Richardson require only one administration of a test. The coefficients reported with the Kuder and Richardson procedures are typically identified as KR-20 or KR-21. The most accurate of these is probably the KR-20 coefficient, but the easiest to calculate is KR-21. However, the KR-21 coefficient assumes that all items in a test are equally difficult, and this is hardly ever the case. Oftentimes both of these values are reported on statistical reports of test results.

If the test items are fairly homogeneous in content (such as all items testing linear equations) and student performance is fairly consistent across all items, the KR-20 coefficient will be about like the Spearman-Brown figure. However, if the test content is quite heterogeneous, the KR-20 value will typically be lower than the Spearman-Brown reliability.

Coefficient Alpha. A third indicator of reliability that instructors will sometimes see is one called *coefficient alpha*. This is a generalized figure that under some conditions matches the split-half and in others matches the KR-20. Alpha can be used when items are not scored dichotomously (right or wrong), so it is useful for essay tests, where students' scores can show a range of values.

Factors That Influence Reliability

We have already noted that the length of the test has an influence on reliability, longer tests being typically more reliable than shorter ones. Here are some additional conditions that affect reliability.

The time limits for a test have an impact on reliability, especially in the split-half and Kuder-Richardson approaches. If some students do not have time to try some items, the proportion of correct responses for those items will decrease and the score spread will increase because some students will not be able to show all they can do. This increase will have a positive, although spurious, influence on the size of the reliability coefficient; that is, the coefficient computed on tests with short time limits tends to be higher than the coefficient computed on tests with ample working time for all students.

The size of the reliability coefficient is also affected by the nature of the group of students from whom the scores are collected. If the group is quite homogeneous in terms of the characteristic being measured, the reliability coefficient of the test will be a lower value than if the group is fairly heterogeneous. The essence of reliability is that two measurements place a student in essentially the same position in the group. If everyone is at about the same score, a very small difference in a person's scores on the two tests could alter that person's position in the group from one test to the other. The wider the spread of scores, other things being equal, the higher the test's reliability, because small differences between an individual's two scores will not markedly alter that person's status in the group from one test to the other.

The difficulty of the test items also affects reliability. We have already noted that traditional test reliability methods depend on a spread of scores. On a very difficult test, there may be very little difference among scores for the bulk of the students.

Everyone will cluster near the bottom of the list of scores. Similarly, on an easy test, many of the students will cluster at the top of the score range. Here we have test scores with very little variability, or spread, and we have just noted that narrow score distributions tend to produce low reliabilities. Faculty will get the best reliabilities on objective tests when about half of the group passes and half fails each item. This is known as 50 percent difficulty for each test item.

Administering and scoring tests also affect reliability. Students should receive a common set of instructions so they all can attack the test under the same conditions. Scoring of the test should be as objective as possible; that is, the same scoring criteria should be applied to each test paper in the same way. The more specific the instructions and the more objective the scoring, the higher the test's reliability.

In summary, faculty should expect the best reliability when their tests are long, but everyone has a chance to try each item; when items are near 50 percent difficulty; when everyone has gotten the same directions for taking the test; and when the test takers have some heterogeneity of ability. As test makers, faculty have control over some of these items, but not others.

Improving Reliability

Now that we have considered features that influence reliability, let us consider how to apply these ideas to tests to increase the faculty's chances of having higher reliabilities. Here is a list of the ways to do it; we discuss the items below.

1. Test should be long enough to sample content well.
2. Time limit should allow most students to finish.
3. Score range should be wide, items at mid-difficulty range.
4. Items should be free of ambiguity and tricks.
5. Directions should be clear and concise.

The tests should be long enough to adequately sample the content. Although there are exceptions, objective tests with fewer than twenty-five to thirty items probably should be avoided. They run the risk of producing low reliabilities.

The time limit on the test should allow everyone (or nearly so) to attempt every item. If not everyone gets this chance, as noted above, the test may appear to be quite reliable, but some of this will be due to rate of work rather than consistency of performance on the content measured by the test. Also, the test will be sampling the skills of the students who finish more completely than the skills of the students who do not get to try some items.

Another way to get higher reliability for the test is to select items that have moderate difficulty. These items have the greatest potential for spreading out the score distribution and for sorting out students who know the content from those who do not. There is a solid statistical reason for this, but it is beyond the scope of this book.

Items should be constructed without ambiguities or tricks to get the students to miss them. Ambiguous items will be interpreted in various ways by different students. These items do not focus on a specific instructional object and consequently do not fit into a sampling plan for our unit of teaching. In testing, faculty are trying to measure what students have achieved with the subject matter, not how trick resistant they are.

To improve the test's reliability, faculty should provide clear and concise directions for taking the test and careful monitoring of the test taking. These features will ensure that all students will understand what the procedures are in taking the test and that any student's score will not be augmented by assistance from colleagues in the class.

Reliability of Essay Tests

The procedures described above apply to objective tests such as multiple-choice and true-false. What about essay tests? Here the big issue appears to be consistency in reading the tests. Faculty will achieve better reliability on scoring essay tests if they write items that are not too broad in scope and if they use a prescribed scoring method (see Chapter Six). Higher reliability in essay tests is also achieved if two readers score the test independently; cases are arbitrated if more than a predetermined discrepancy appears in scores between the two readers. Admittedly, two readers are not always available, so it is doubly important to write questions that clearly point the students toward a task that is not too broad and to employ a prescribed reading method.

Standard Error of Measurement

Computer analyses of objective test results will often include a figure called the *standard error of measurement,* a term that tells faculty about imprecisions in their test data.

Imagine once again that a graduate assistant is making repeated measurements of the width of an office with a cloth tape measure. Sometimes the tape is stretched tightly during the measurement, and sometimes the tape is a little slack. The instructor notices that the measurements vary, due to imprecision that arises from the flexibility of the tape measure and the graduate assistant's variable tugging on the tape as he works. Sometimes the measurement underestimates the width of the room; sometimes it overestimates it. In other words, the measurements are not perfectly reliable. While the graduate assistant replicates the procedure, the instructor notices that the measurements, when graphed, form a narrow, bell-shaped curve. The *mean* (the arithmetic average) of this set of measurements is probably the "true" width of the room. If the instructor calculates a *standard deviation* for the set of measurements, the value can be used to say how far from the true value any one measurement is likely to be. The standard deviation also allows the instructor to lay out a range within which the true measurement is likely to fall.

In test data, instructors have only one score for each person. That score may, or may not, be accurate (the lower the reliability of the test, the more inaccurate the score is expected to be). However, the standard error allows the instructor to lay out a range within which the student's true score is likely to lie.

For example, suppose on a sixty-item test Jill gets a score of 45. The instructor reads on the computer analysis of the test that the standard error is 1.5. That means 1.5 score points. From the normal, bell-shaped curve we know that between the mean and one standard error above the mean fall 34 percent of the scores, and 34 percent more fall between the mean and one standard error below the mean; that is, there are 68 chances in 100 of any given score being within (plus or minus) one standard error of the true score.

Now go back to Jill, who had a test score of 45. Jill's true score is very likely (68 chances out of 100) to be in the range of 45 plus or minus 1.5 points (the standard error). It tells us to expect her true score to be in the range of 43.5 to 46.5.

Since no test is perfectly reliable, any given score on the test is likely to deviate a few points from the student's true score. Some scores will contain more inaccuracy than others. Some will be overestimates, some underestimates, but most (68 percent) will likely be within one standard error of the true score. Therefore, the standard error helps an instructor interpret the test's reliability in terms of actual score data. The lower the test's reliability, the larger the standard error and the wider the range within which an instructor will expect a student's true score to fall. For this reason, all test users want to do whatever they can to achieve high reliability and small standard errors of measurement. (The standard error of measurement is calculated as $SEM = s\sqrt{(1 - r)}$, where s is the test standard deviation, and r is the reliability coefficient.)

Test Validity

When an observer measures something, it is reasonable to expect that the measurement will provide information that helps the observer make decisions about the object being measured. A measurement can be consistent, that is, reliable, but not give observers information that will improve their decisions about the focal object. For example, an individual measures the specific gravity of a water sample several times and gets the same result each time. The measurement is highly reliable. But the measurement is not useful if that person wants to determine the bacterial count of the sample. The procedure has reliability but not validity. That is, the procedure is consistent but not relevant to the problem at hand, namely, the purity of the water.

A test is valid if it provides data that increase the accuracy of decisions about a person or object. Tests do not have general validity; they are valid in relation to a specific variable, such as intelligence, achievement of course objectives, or test anxiety.

Evidence for test validity is established in several ways. In this book we are interested in the educational use of tests, so we confine our discussion to one type of evidence while giving passing attention to other types.

The obvious way to collect evidence of a test's validity is to compare students' scores on a test to some external measure of the same trait that the test measures. For example, a test for mechanical aptitude could be validated by comparing students' scores on the test with grades those students make in a course in auto mechanics. If the test is valid as a measure of mechanical aptitude, students' scores on the test should correspond with students' progress in the course. The data here are criterion-related because they relate test scores to a measure of the variable we wish to predict with the test. We are looking at criterion-related evidence when we correlate Scholastic Aptitude Test scores with freshman grades.

A second way to establish the validity of a test is common in studies of abstract psychological traits, such as risk taking, persistence, paranoia, and so on. Here a test is built to put people in rank order on some abstract trait called a construct. A *construct* is a hypothesized trait postulated because observers see a set of apparently related behaviors that seem to characterize a single concept. Intelligence is a construct. People who show facility in solving abstract problems, in using number concepts, in manipulating objects in space, and on related tasks are exhibiting behaviors that characterize the single construct of intelligence. If people who most often demonstrate the behaviors that characterize the construct get the highest scores on the test claiming to measure intelligence, we believe we have construct-related evidence of the test's validity.

We mention validation based on criterion-related and construct-related data only because these methods are often seen in the literature. In this book we are interested only in content-related validation. In this case, the validity of a test is based on how adequately it samples a domain of behavior or knowledge about which we will make an inference.

At this point, faculty should remind themselves that tests are not a measure of an entire domain but are samples of the desired behavior — samples from which instructors will make conclusions about how students stand on the entire domain. Because there are often problems with sampling, faculty should have a carefully planned sampling procedure so that conclusions (here typically ending in course grades) will be made with confidence.

Briefly, content validation procedures consist of laying out the content of the domain in a systematic way and building the test to sample this domain appropriately. We look at each of these steps separately as they pertain to validating instructor-made classroom tests in a given course of study.

Building a Course Blueprint

If, on a test, an instructor samples the course objectives in proportion to their importance in the course, the instructor's test will have content validity. To lay out the course objectives in a systematic manner, a table of specifications is needed. We discussed the concept of a table of specifications in Chapter Two, and described Bloom's taxonomy of educational objectives as a guide for establishing levels of cognitive demand. Now we capitalize on our presentation in Chapter Two to lay out a blueprint for a test that will have content validity.

Here is how it works. On the horizontal dimension of the table we list the cognitive levels of the course content, while on the vertical dimension we lay out the course topics. The body of the table then teases out the topics into the cognitive levels across the horizontal dimension. Tables 3.1 and 3.2 are two examples of tables of specifications in quite different disciplines, biology and literature.

Although Bloom has described six levels of cognitive complexity, we have used only three in our tables. Because the processes of analysis, synthesis, and evaluation (the top three levels in Bloom's taxonomy) are so intertwined, it is very hard to differentiate these operations. Therefore, we have combined

Table 3.1. A Table of Specifications for a Unit on the Amoeba.

Amoeba Content	Cognitive Objectives		
	Knowledge/ Comprehension	Application	Higher-Level Skills
Classification	Phylum, others in phylum (3)		Provide characteristics of organism, classify protozoa or not (2)
Structure	Cell parts, functions (5)	Relating environ- ment to impact on cell parts (2)	
Reproduction	Steps in fission, factors influenc- ing (3)		Compare sets of factors in terms of promoting reproduction (2)
Medical effects	Effects of *Entamoeba histolytica* (2)	Solving medical problems tied to amoeba (2)	Reduce health risks, identify relevant variables (3)
	13	4	7

them into one higher-level category to simplify the table. We have also combined the knowledge category with comprehension to create the level of lowest cognitive demand.

In Table 3.1, the three cognitive operations condensed from Bloom are listed along the top of the table. Then the first course topic, classification, is listed, and across that row we have objectives at the knowledge/comprehension level and at the higher level. Generic examples of the objectives are given to guide instructors' thinking while they are writing examination questions. Also listed are the number of items we believe will cover these topics at each level. For the topic classification, there are three test items at the knowledge/comprehension level and two at the higher level.

Having sorted the objectives for the classification topic, instructors turn to the next course topic, structure, and again sort out the objectives. This procedure continues until instructors have covered the unit of instruction for which they are preparing an examination. At that point, faculty have a plan that will guide them along the topics in the unit and will steer their test writing not just to lower-level content but also to the more cognitively demanding features of the content.

An example of a table of specifications in a different discipline is given in Table 3.2. In this table of specifications, we have a quite different subject, but there is something at each cognitive level to be assessed in most, if not all, instructional topics. This is one of the strong points of a table of specifications. It points to each aspect of instruction and consequently to each operation for which instructors must write at least one item for the test. If a section of the table is filled in, instructors are indeed obligated to write the appropriate number of test items to cover that topic at the specified level. If they do not write them, their test fails to adequately sample the domain and, therefore, loses some of its validity.

A table of specifications not only provides a blueprint for assessing instructional outcomes but also guides teaching. It is assumed that the table emerges out of teaching, but once having put the table together, the instructor can use it as a format

Table 3.2. A Table of Specifications for a Unit on the Sonnet.

| Sonnet Content | Cognitive Objectives | | |
	Knowledge/ Comprehension	Application	Higher-Level Skills
Define	Single concept, number of lines, rhyme (3)		
Parts	Octave, sestet, quatrains, rhyme pattern (5)	Given set of lines, break into format; write a sonnet (2)	Given poem, identify "errors" in terms of sonnet (2)
Forms	Petrarchan, English (2)	Construct a sonnet to match a form (2)	
Identify	Identify ten "well-known" sonnets by author (3)		Given a "sonnet," analyze to identify with author (2)
	13	4	4

for instructional planning. Once faculty have constructed a table of specifications, they should adhere fairly closely to it. However, it should be their tool, not their overseer. If they decide to alter their instructional plan by dropping or adding a topic or giving more or less time to a concept, they should simply change the table of specifications. The table should follow instruction as well as lead it.

The intent is to make tests correspond to teaching objectives, and a table of specifications is the prescribed way of doing this. By using a table of specifications as a guide to sampling the content and the cognitive objectives, the instructor will be able to write a test that has content validity.

Reliability and Validity

No matter how carefully an instructor develops a sample of the instructional domain, the test cannot be valid unless it is first reliable. Unless test scores rank a student in the group consistently, faculty cannot make reasonable inferences about that student's mastery of the test's domain. Consequently, instructors will want to pay considerable attention to the reliability of the test. Everything else depends on that quality.

Validity and Criterion-Referenced Tests

Although the purpose of criterion-referenced tests is different from that of norm-referenced tests, the validation procedures are essentially the same for both. In both cases faculty should be very much concerned that their tests be an appropriate sample of the skills, knowledge, and so on, that they are promoting through instruction. In criterion-referenced tests, however, faculty want to see that students perform up to criterion in each of the topics listed on the table of specifications. Instructors will write their items to be at criterion level, although the items should follow the types and numbers as sorted out in the table of specifications. In norm-referenced tests, we are not constrained by a set criterion level. The difference is in the item construction, not in the layout of content or the sampling procedure.

Factors That Affect Validity

The careful sampling of content and mental functions is the heart of the validation of instructor-made classroom tests. However, no matter how carefully an instructor tries to lay out the course content, or how carefully the sampling of the content is done, several additional factors can invalidate a test. Here are the most common of these factors:

1. Directions are not clear.
2. Test requires inappropriate levels of skills that are not part of course objectives.
3. Test items are poorly written.
4. Test length does not allow adequate sampling of content.
5. Complexity and subjectivity of scoring inaccurately rank some students.

The directions for taking the test should be clearly stated. If students misinterpret the directions and fail to respond in the way the instructor intended, the test will not adequately assess student achievement. Clear directions are essential so that all students know exactly what they are expected to do with the test materials.

The test should focus on the skills the instructor has taught and wishes to assess. Other skills should not be allowed to materially complicate this task. For example, suppose the objective involves the interpretation of research data. The instructor begins the test by first asking students to read a research article. Then the test directions ask them to interpret a number of items in the body of the article. In completing the task, slow readers will be penalized because they will have less time to do a careful job of interpretation and analysis of the article. The test is evaluating students on a task not taught as part of the objectives, namely, reading skill. As a result, the instructor will conclude that some students cannot do the task, even though without the heavy reading demand, or with more time, they might have; consequently, the instructor loses some validity for the test.

Badly constructed test items also reduce test validity. Even if an instructor has the appropriate number of items at each cell on the table of specifications, if any one of those items is poorly constructed, that topic will not be adequately represented among other topics in the instructional plan. Items that are inappropriately easy or hard, ambiguous, or that do not assess the cognitive level for which they are intended will reduce the validity of the test as an acceptable sample of the instructional domain.

The length of the test is another factor that affects the content validity. The test should be long enough to complete the sampling as laid out in the table of specifications. However, it should not be so long that many students will not have a chance to finish. If it is, the instructor does not know how students would have performed on the unfinished items in the test, and their scores will indicate they did not know the content when, in fact, they may have known much of it if time had allowed them to get to it. In other words, the instructor is projecting the students to be at a point on the knowledge continuum which is inaccurate in terms of their actual knowledge level. A test that is too long can invalidate the instructor's ability to make inferences about a student's status.

Complexity and subjectivity of scoring also affect a test's validity. If scoring has many steps or is otherwise complex, there are many opportunities to make mistakes and report an inaccurate (and invalid) score. Also, if scoring is subjective and easily influenced by factors that are not part of the teaching objectives, scores may not represent a student's true status in the skills and knowledge instructors are trying to assess.

In sum, the layout and sampling of the domain is an important step in achieving content validity. However, faculty must attend to a number of nuisance variables if their tests are going to have validity.

Summary

In this chapter, we discussed two focal concepts in testing—indeed, in all measurements—reliability and validity. The principal ideas are summarized in the following statements:

1. Reliability indicates the extent to which the two parallel measures agree as to the rank of students in the group. We express this relationship between two measurements as a correlation coefficient, an indicator of correspondence ranging from 0 (no relationship between the two measurements) to 1.00 (the cases rank exactly on the second measurement as they did on the first). Most pairs of measurements correlate somewhere between these extremes, but we shoot for correlations of, say, .75 or more for the reliabilities on classroom tests.

2. Several factors influence test reliability. Most prominent among the positive influences are adequate test length to sample the course content well, sufficient time for all to finish, a moderate level of difficulty, and clear directions.

3. We know that a test may not precisely identify the student's "true" ability, so psychometricians have devised the standard error, the score range within which the true score is expected to fall. The higher the reliability for a test, the narrower this range. The standard error helps faculty identify the accuracy of their students' test scores.

4. Validity is the extent to which the test data aid faculty in making decisions about a person in terms of a given variable, such as course achievement. Although there are several types of validity data, the one academicians are mainly interested in is content-related validity. To achieve validity, the instructor lays out the instructional content in a systematic way, using a table of specifications, and then uses the table to build the test. The test should sample the course objectives in proportion to their importance in the course.

5. Criterion-referenced tests should be built around course content in the same fashion that norm-referenced tests are. The difference is that in criterion-referenced tests faculty have a given level of performance at which they are aiming the items, above which they declare the performance is adequate, below which it is inadequate. The structuring of the test around a table of specifications is appropriate in all cases to ensure validity.

6. There are several factors that affect test validity positively. Most notable among these are adequate and appropriate content sampling in the test and avoidance of nonfocal skills (such as heavy reading in a mathematics test), clear directions,

well-written test items, and less complex and subjective scoring. In sum, if faculty tests are going to achieve what faculty expect them to — that is, rank students in accordance with their true status in achieving course objectives — test writers must attend to the qualities of validity and reliability. Without both of these qualities, a test will provide erroneous information on which to base inferences about student learning. Instructors wish to avoid that, so they will want to pursue reliability and validity at all points in the development and application of their tests.

4

Multiple-Choice Items

Multiple-choice items are the most widely used selection-type item in the college classroom; thus it is very important that faculty learn to write them well. The popularity of multiple-choice items lies in their versatility; they can measure a wide range of content and learning outcomes. Nitko says: "Among the various types of response choice items, the multiple-choice item can be used to test a greater variety of instructional objectives" (1983, p. 193). Some college instructors, however, are reluctant to use multiple-choice items because they believe that these items measure only superficial learning. That certainly does not have to be the case. Properly constructed multiple-choice items can measure the higher-level cognitive objectives such as analysis and evaluation as well as the lower knowledge level. These items also permit a wide sampling of content, which is important to the content-related validity of classroom tests.

Multiple-choice items are especially beneficial in large lecture classes, because most professors do not have the time to grade hundreds of essay tests. Multiple-choice tests can be scored

Note: The authors are indebted to the following professors at Indiana University for sharing test items from their files: Dr. Laura Ginger, business law; Dr. John Lovell, political science; Dr. Phillip Saunders, economics; Dr. Michael Tansey, biology; Dr. Robert Wicks, journalism; Dr. Allen Winold, music; and to Peter M. Jacobs, teaching assistant in geography at University of Wisconsin, Madison.

quickly by machine; thus students can receive feedback generally by the next class meeting.

While scoring is quick and easy, the preparation of a multiple-choice test is not. It takes a great deal of time, effort, and creativity to write good multiple-choice items, especially those that measure higher-level objectives. Most professional item writers are able to write only three or four items per day. It is certainly not possible to sit down the night before a scheduled exam and write a collection of effective multiple-choice items. It takes time to develop problems that require students to think rather than to recall, time to think of plausible distractors (incorrect options), and time to revise items. When time is limited, instructors often end up with items that measure only recall of factual knowledge because these are the easiest to write.

Semb and Spencer (1976) surveyed seventeen University of Kansas faculty members in various disciplines about the type of test items they write. These instructors report that about one-third of their test questions measure their students' complex cognitive skills. Careful categorization by independent judges showed that only 8.5 percent of the test items actually used by these instructors required complex skills; the remaining 91.5 percent required only recall or recognition. The judges concluded that "many instructors are testing mainly over recall tasks . . . what is disturbing is that they do not even know it" (Semb and Spencer, 1976, p. 121).

The best method is to write a few multiple-choice items each week, perhaps some after each lecture. This procedure helps not only to focus on the important points covered in each lecture but also to spread out the working time needed to prepare the test. Putting the items on a personal computer greatly facilitates revision of the items.

The greatest effort in test writing is required the first time instructors teach a course. Once instructors have written good items, they can save them and gradually accumulate a file of items that can be sampled for future exams (assuming the content and objectives remain the same). The test file can be saved on index cards or preferably on a computer disk. We recommend that a few new items be written each time a test is used. Item analysis (discussed in a later chapter) permits the instructor to identify items that are worth maintaining in the test file.

How should faculty go about writing good multiple-choice items? First, they need to look at effective ways for developing this type of test item, and then they should follow accepted guidelines for writing them so that they are clear and unambiguous.

Anatomy of Multiple-Choice Items

The multiple-choice item consists of a stimulus, called the *stem,* and a number of possible responses, including the correct or best answer plus three or four distractors.

Stem

The criterion of a well-written stem is that students are able to read the stem and formulate a tentative answer even before reading the options. The stem may be an incomplete sentence or a question. An example of an item that has an incomplete sentence as the stem is:

Of the following coefficients of correlation, the one with the least predictive value is

a.   .17
b.   − .23
c.   .50
d.   .91
e.   − 1.00

The same item with the stem in the form of a question would be written:

Which one of the following coefficients of correlation has the least predictive value?

a.   .17
b.   − .23
c.   .50
d.   .91
e.   − 1.00

Experts do not agree that one format is superior to the other. Use whichever presents the problem most clearly and unambiguously to the student. In either format, however, the stem must present a problem that focuses on some important concept or principle in the course. Instructors should not test on trivial details or obscure facts hidden in the fine print. The instructor's aim is not to trick students but to determine if they have learned the important points. One of the most common student complaints about tests is that they measure trivial information not indicative of the material stressed in the course. Such tests are probably written because instructors lack the time required to develop items at the higher levels of Bloom's taxonomy. As we pointed out earlier, low-level questions measuring factual knowledge are much easier to write.

Distractors

The alternatives following the multiple-choice stem consist of the correct answer plus three or four *plausible* distractors. The distractors may be complete sentences, phrases, or single words. Four alternatives per item is probably the most popular format, and we recommend writing at least four options unless doing so means adding an implausible option. It is not absolutely necessary that every item in the test have the same number of options, but it might be perplexing to students if the number of options varies.

Writing distractors is probably the most important and difficult part of building multiple-choice items. Distractors should be fabricated from common errors that students make or misconceptions they may have. One useful strategy in generating distractors is to phrase an item in the form of a completion or a short-answer question. Think of the incorrect responses that students would be likely to make to the question, and let these be the distractors in the multiple-choice item. Experienced instructors generally know what the students' errors and misconceptions are likely to be. For example, in writing items for a statistics test, we know the typical procedural errors students make in the process of solving problems. Each distractor can be an answer that students would get if they made those errors.

Or if time is available, instructors might even give a short-answer quiz over the material to obtain students' wrong answers.

Writing effective multiple-choice questions is always difficult, but the following guidelines will help instructors write better items. Some of these guidelines may appear self-evident, but the principles put forth are very important to producing effective multiple-choice tests. Simple examples will be used to illustrate each point.

Guidelines for Writing Multiple-Choice Items

1. The stem should present the problem in the simplest form consistent with precision and clarity. To make sure that the stem presents a problem, always include a *verb* in the statement. While the stem should contain all the information essential to understanding the problem, it should not be padded with superfluous material. Some instructors may think that extra verbiage adds to the complexity of the item, but, in fact, padding only adds to the students' reading time. The following two examples illustrate poorly written stems and ways to improve them:

Example A: The mean

a. Is the most frequently occurring score in a distribution
b. Corresponds to the 50th percentile in the distribution
c. Is the arithmetic average of the scores
d. Is the measure of central tendency least influenced by the value of each score

The above stem is defective because it does not contain a verb and hence does not present a problem. The stem should be reworded to present a problem to the student. It would be better to write the item as follows:

The mean of a distribution of test scores is the

a. Most frequently occurring score
b. 50th percentile
c. Arithmetic average

d.   Measure of central tendency least influenced by the value
     of each score

Example B: A university developed an aptitude test to use for
admission to its Honors Program. The test was administered
to a group of applicants to the Honors Program and analysis
of the results indicated that the reliability of the aptitude test
was .80. The university admissions office had been interested
in having a new aptitude test for all applicants, so later the aptitude test was administered to all applicants to the university.
The results for the larger group were analyzed. What would
you expect the reliability coefficient of the test to be, based on
the latter analysis?

a.   Above .80
b.   Below .80
c.   .80
d.   Impossible to determine from the information given

     The above stem contains too much unnecessary material.
It could be restated much more concisely and still test knowledge of the very same principle:

An aptitude test administered to a group of applicants to an
Honors Program had a reliability of .80. What would you expect the reliability coefficient to be if the test were administered
to all the applicants to the university?

a.   Above .80
b.   Below .80
c.   .80
d.   Impossible to determine from information given

     2. As a corollary to the above guideline, instructors should
avoid unnecessary repetition of material in the options by including as much of the item as possible in the stem. That is, do not
repeat words in each option that could be put in the stem one
time. Following this guideline not only saves time for the typist but

also saves reading time for students. The following poorly constructed item and its improved version illustrate this point:

Which of the following is the best definition of sociobiology?

a. The scientific study of humans and their relationships within the environment
b. The scientific study of animal societies and communication
c. The scientific study of plants and their reproductive processes
d. The scientific study of plants and their effect on other species
e. The scientific study of the number of species in existence

Sociobiology is the scientific study of

a. Humans and their relationships within the environment
b. Animal societies and communications
c. Plants and their reproductive processes
d. Plants and their effect on other species
e. The number of species in existence

3. After writing the stem, it is best to write the correct response first and then the distractors. Writing the correct response first ensures that adequate attention is given to formulating the one *correct* or clearly *best* answer for the question. At the same time, the test writer must be certain that there is only *one* correct or clearly best answer. This rule seems very obvious, but occasionally, without careful checking, instructors will include an item with more than one correct answer. For instance, the instructor may have said something in lecture that does not agree with what is in the text, so students could argue about the keyed response.

In the directions to a multiple-choice test, instructors must tell students whether they are to select the *correct* or the *best* answer. If the students are to select the "correct" answer, it must be correct beyond any question. Correct answers should be used only in situations where there are absolute standards of correctness, such as in mathematics, grammar, statistics, or spelling tests. Otherwise, students should be instructed to select the "best" answer. The best answer should be the one that knowledgeable people agree on. We prefer the best-answer format in most cases. When students are instructed to select the correct answer, they can often argue that another answer is also correct. But when this happens with the best-answer format, the instructor can say that while another answer may have an element of truth, it is not the best of the answers offered in that particular situation. Thus, the best-answer format helps to reduce arguments between instructors and students. The following example violates the principle of one best or correct answer:

The function of the hypothesis in a research study is to provide

a.   Tentative explanation of phenomena
b.   Proven explanation of phenomena
c.   Framework for interpretation of the findings
d.   Direction for the research

      There is no single best or correct answer among the options. The options would need to be reworded so that only one is clearly best or correct. What do instructors do if they find they have violated this guideline in one of their tests? They can either omit the item from the scoring process or they can accept either answer as correct.

      4. The distractors that are written must be incorrect, but they should have enough plausibility to attract the students who do not know the material very well. It is often difficult to come up with three or four reasonable distractors, so instructors will add one or two that are not really plausible. But if the poorly prepared student is not attracted to these options, they might as well not be included because they are not serving any measurement purpose. Consider the following example:

The 1989 announcement that controlled nuclear fusion could be effected in a basic laboratory experiment at room temperature was made by

a. Watson and Crick
b. Pons and Fleischmann
c. Einstein and Teller
d. Koch and Jenner
e. Fermi and Mueller

While the first two options are plausible, the last three are not. These three options should be replaced with ones containing the names of contemporary scientists. If a sufficient number of plausible options cannot be written, then it is best to eliminate that question from the test.

Instructors should also avoid writing absurd distractors. In an attempt to be humorous, some instructors include distractors that are ludicrous. The students may find the distractor funny, but they obviously will not choose it, so it serves no measurement purpose and trivializes the testing process. What about putting humor into test items? Some faculty like to use humorous items because they believe that humor encourages students to relax a bit and see the test in a less stressful context. McMorris, Urbach, and Connor (1985) investigate the effect of including humor in tests. They find that the inclusion of humorous items has no real effect on test performance but that students like the humorous items and think they are easier. If instructors want to incorporate some humor into the test, they should put it in the stem of the question rather than in the distractors. A humorous distractor is too likely to be ignored by students. The following item illustrates this point:

The famous World War II journalist who was killed on Iwo Jima was

a. Jim Nabors
b. Gomer Pyle
c. Ernie Pyle
d. Goober Pyle
e. Jim Carter

In an attempt to be humorous, the writer included some absurd options that make the item worthless. Options (a), (b), (d), and (e) should be replaced with the names of other World War II journalists, such as Edward R. Murrow, Eric Sevareid, Walter Cronkite, and so on.

The difficulty of test items can be increased by making the distractors more homogeneous. The more homogeneous the options, the more discrimination required on the part of the students and the more difficult the item. If a couple of the options are clearly different from the others, then students can easily eliminate them from consideration.

5. Avoid giving irrelevant clues to the answer. Students' responses are sometimes based not on what they have learned but rather on some clues they find in the stem or distractors. Poorly constructed items that measure students' test-taking skills rather than their learning are a serious drawback of multiple-choice tests. Test-wise students' use of these clues gives them an advantage over other less sophisticated students, reducing the validity of the test for measuring students' knowledge. There are several types of clues that enable students to give the correct answer without really having the knowledge.

• *Length clue.* The longest option is often the correct one because the writer has excessively qualified the information to ensure it is correct. Students learn quickly that the longest response is often the correct one. If the correct answer must be very long, then instructors should try to make at least one of the incorrect options approximately the same length. Or they should occasionally make an incorrect option longer than the others so that students cannot depend on length as a clue to the correct answer. Consider the following example:

Good science and good scientists can be characterized in certain ways. Which one of the following is *not* a characteristic of good science or good scientists?

a.   Willingness to submit to peer review
b.   Willingness to publish details of methodology so that experiments or observations can be repeated by others

c.   Creativity: ability to have many ideas and then select the best
d.   Infallibility: recognition that science is correct, and acceptance that, once presented, experimental data and observations are beyond criticism by other scientists
e.   Valuing the search for truth, in and of itself

The correct answer is (d); its longer length would definitely be a clue.

   • *Verbal association clue.* Avoid writing items in which a verbal association can be made between the stem and the correct option. Consider the following example:

Cultivation analysis refers to

a.   A mathematical formula designed to identify specific audience segments
b.   The specific techniques utilized by Arbitron and Nielson in data collection procedures
c.   The notion that media usage tends to cultivate perceptions of reality consistent with the view of the world presented in television news
d.   A statistical technique similar to factor analysis
e.   A means of building viewership by "giving the audience what it wants"

   Different forms of the same word appear in the stem and in the correct option. The use of *cultivation* in the stem and *cultivate* in option (c) would definitely serve as a clue to the correctness of that option. The correct option is also longer than the others, providing another clue. This item might be improved by making the distractors longer and eliminating the word *cultivate* from the correct response. Or we might keep the word *cultivate* in option (c) while also using it in an incorrect option, for example in (e): "A means of cultivating viewership . . . "

   • *Grammatical clue.* The options must complete a grammatically correct statement. If not, clues are provided to the right answer. Consider the following example:

The coefficient of correlation found by correlating students' scores on a classroom social studies test with their scores on a standardized social studies test is called a

a.   Validity coefficient
b.   Index of reliability
c.   Equivalence coefficient
d.   Equivalence and stability coefficient
e.   Internal consistency coefficient

   Option (a) is the only one that is grammatically consistent with the stem. It could be correctly selected without knowing anything about the content. This grammatical clue can be eliminated by including both articles, a and an, in the stem. For example, "The coefficient of correlation . . . is called a(n) . . . "
   • *Specific determiners.* Avoid the use of specific determiners, those "modifying words or phrases that limit the meaning of sentences or cause the meaning to be true or false only in extreme cases" (Osterling, 1989, p. 166). Test-wise students are quick to detect these words and use them as clues to the correct answer. For example, words such as *all, never,* and *always* are generally found in incorrect options. Words such as *usually, sometimes, typically,* and *maybe* are more likely to be found in the correct option.
   6. Use positive statements if possible. Negative statements can be confusing for students to interpret. Furthermore, due to the pressure of a test, students who know the material can easily overlook the negative and mark the item wrong. If negative wording is used, call attention to it by underlining, capitalizing, or using boldface letters.

The state that is <u>not</u> south of the Mason-Dixon line is

a.   Alabama
b.   Florida
c.   Kentucky
d.   Maryland
e.   Vermont

A positively stated item tests the same concept and would be less confusing to students.

The state that is north of the Mason-Dixon line is

a. Alabama
b. Florida
c. Kentucky
d. Maryland
e. Vermont

7. Use options such as "all of the above" and "none of the above" rarely. Instructors often use one or the other of these options because it reduces the number of distractors they have to write. Items with "all of the above" as a distractor are generally too easy. If students can recognize that just one answer is incorrect, then they can eliminate the option "all of the above" from consideration. By contrast, if students can recognize that at least two of the options are correct, they would automatically select the "all of the above" option. In either case, students can get the answer right on the basis of incomplete information. Furthermore, when "all of the above" is used, it is too often the correct response. Students who are quick to see this may choose the option automatically when they are not sure of the correct answer. Mentzer (1982) examined thirty-five files of multiple-choice test items for evidence of biases in the correct answers. The most frequently occurring bias is the "all of the above" response, in which that answer is correct significantly more than 25 percent of the time. It is acceptable to use "all of the above" in situations where the instructor wants to determine if students have learned all the relevant characteristics or attributes of some phenomenon. But if it is used, make sure it is not always or usually the correct response. Occasionally use it as an incorrect response.

"None of the above" (NA) is a rather controversial distractor; a number of research studies have investigated its use as an option in multiple-choice items. Most researchers conclude that it should be used only rarely and in certain circumstances. It should be used only with the correct-answer format, that is, when absolute standards of correctness can be applied, as in mathematics, statistics, mechanics of grammar, geography, historical dates, and spelling. Otherwise, students can argue about the correctness of one or more of the other options. It should *not* be used with negatively stated stems, because NA plus the negative in the stem creates a double negative that is confusing to students. "None of the above" is rarely used for the correct answer, so its credibility as an option suffers. If NA is used, it should be the correct option in approximately 25 percent of the items in which it appears. And instructors should use it as the correct option early in the test so that students will have to consider it as a plausible distractor. Some instructors object to using NA as a correct option because such questions do not provide the correct answer for students to see and therefore do not reinforce the correct answer.

Some of the research on NA has focused on whether this option makes items more difficult. Rich and Johanson (1990) studied the effect of NA on test items' difficulty and ability to discriminate between students of high and low achievement. They found that using NA makes the item more difficult and more discriminating than using a weak distractor. Their recommendation is that NA be used only to improve items not having an optimal difficulty level. That is, if analysis shows that the item is too easy, substitute NA for one of the conventional but weak distractors.

Frary (1991) investigated the use of the NA option in college-level tests for large classes in eight academic disciplines. He finds that when compared to the average item not containing NA, the average NA item is slightly more difficult but almost equally discriminating. Items for which NA is the correct answer are, on average, slightly more difficult than items for which NA is a distractor. But the two types of items are almost equal in their ability to discriminate between students. Frary concludes that NA can be used as an option in classroom tests, especially for items that would otherwise be too easy.

8. Make certain that each multiple-choice item is independent. Getting the correct answer to one item should not be contingent upon getting the correct response to other items. At the

same time, avoid letting one item provide a clue to the answer to another item.

9. Arrange the options in a logical order if possible. For example, arrange options that are numbers in ascending order, put single words in alphabetical order, and list dates chronologically. If there is no logical order, randomize so as to avoid patterns in the correct responses. Instructors often have preferences for placing the correct answer in a certain position, such as the middle. But the correct answers should be divided approximately evenly over the four or five options. Mentzer's (1982) research shows that option (a) is underutilized as the correct response. In other words, it is not the correct response approximately 25 percent of the time in tests with four alternatives. Option (c) is overutilized as the correct response; it is the correct response more than 25 percent of the time in four-option items. In a study of high school students, Carter (1986) finds that students often ignore option (d) because they say it is funny or ridiculous.

10. If an item contains controversial material, cite the authority whose opinion is being used in the question. For example, use phrases like "According to my lecture," "As stated by the text," "In Freud's opinion," and so on.

11. When writing item stems and options, avoid lifting statements verbatim from the text. Using textbook excerpts encourages students to memorize. If instructors rephrase or create new situations and examples, they can determine whether or not students really understand the material.

12. Arranging the options in a vertical column makes reading easier and is much less confusing than options written horizontally across the page. The options should be written in grammatically parallel form whenever possible; that is, do not begin one option with a verb, another with a gerund, another with an adjective, and so on.

Developing Test Items

There is no magic formula for writing multiple-choice items. It is, as we pointed out earlier, a challenging and time-consuming task. The item writer must be thoroughly versed in a content area and know the important concepts and principles that should be tested. Knowing the misconceptions that students have and the errors they make helps one to write good distractors. The content of the items comes from the thoughtfulness and creativity of the writer. As Wesman writes, "Every test item begins with an idea in the mind of the item writer . . . there is no automatic process for the production of item ideas. They must be invented or discovered, and in these processes chance thoughts and in- spirations are very important" (1971, p. 86). If instructors are trying to measure higher-level thinking processes, it is especially important to develop novel or thought-provoking situations. While it is true that items have to be invented, there are some strategies that can be employed to help item writers develop mul- tiple-choice items.

Techniques

The following techniques can be used to build items.

- p ——→ c. A premise (p) presented in the stem is followed by a particular consequence (c) in one of the options.

  Example: If nominal gross national product (GNP) increases at a rate of 10 percent per year while the GNP deflator in- creases at 8 percent per year, then real GNP

  a. Remains constant
  b. Rises by 10 percent
  c. Falls by 8 percent
  d. Rises by 2 percent

- p + p ——→ c. Two or more premises in combination lead to a particular conclusion.

  Example: If the GNP in current dollars was $360 billion in 1955 and $450 billion in 1963, and the appropriate price index (1950 = 100) was 120 in 1955 and 125 in 1963, then it can be concluded that between 1955 and 1963 real GNP

a.   Increased by about $60 billion
b.   Increased by about $94 billion
c.   Increased by about $100 billion
d.   Increased by about $117 billion
e.   Decreased by about $32 billion

• Analogy a : b = c : d. A pair of words with a precise relationship is presented; the student must select the answer choice containing a pair of words whose relationship is closest to that of the given pair.

Example: Editor is to newspaper as _____ is to TV.

a.   News director
b.   Business manager
c.   Associate producer
d.   Assignment editor

• Classification of terms, names, statements.

Example: B. F. Skinner would be classified as a

a.   Behaviorist
b.   Functionalist
c.   Gestaltist
d.   Structuralist

• Two propositions are presented in the stem. The testee must decide whether both are true, neither is true, (a) but not (b) is true, (b) but not (a) is true.

Example: A biologist grinds up three frogs, two shrubs, and one undergraduate in a big blender and isolates a catalyst from the resulting mixture. The biologist purifies the catalyst and then assays it for its chemical composition. The catalyst is composed *solely* of carbon, hydrogen, oxygen, and iron. The catalyst must therefore be a/an (a) enzyme (b) protein.

a. (a) but not (b)
b. (b) but not (a)
c. Both (a) and (b)
d. Neither (a) nor (b)

• Context-dependent item set. An item set presents a stimulus (a written scenario, graph, map, picture, table containing data, newspaper article) that is followed by a series of
multiple-choice items based on the stimulus. There may be
five to ten multiple-choice items in a set. The item set is an
excellent way to measure high-level cognitive skills, such as
comprehension, analysis, and application. Haladyna (1992)
said that because the item set is a unit containing a number
of responses, it provides valuable information about the quality of the learning experience upon which the item set is
based. But it is essential that the material presented in the
stimulus be novel or else it might simply measure knowledge or recall.

Example: Assume an economy is producing only one product.
Output and price data for a five-year period are as follows.
Answer the next three questions on the basis of these data.

Year	Units of output	Price per unit
1	3	$3
2	4	4
3	6	5
4	7	7
5	8	8

1. If year 3 is chosen as the base year, the price index for
    year 1

    a. Is 40 percent
    b. Is 60 percent
    c. Is 140 percent
    d. Is 167 percent
    e. Cannot be determined from the information
        given

2. The money GNP for year 4

    a. Is $35
    b. Is $40
    c. Is $49
    d. Is $55
    e. Cannot be determined from the information given

3. Real GNP for year 5

    a. Is $40
    b. Is $49
    c. Is $64
    d. Is $160
    e. Cannot be determined from the information given

Sources

A useful source of multiple-choice items is the collection of items contained in the instructor's manual that comes with many textbooks. Instructors need to critically examine these items before using them in their tests. The items in these manuals often measure only knowledge and may not be well written, but at least they may provide ideas for items that can be rewritten in an improved form. To illustrate, the following is an item taken from an instructor's manual:

A percentile score is the

a. Percentage of items a student answers correctly
b. Percentage of students that answer an item correctly
c. Percentage of a group getting a lower score
d. Average score for a group on a test

The above item tests only the students' recall of the definition of a percentile. An improved item measuring the same concept would be the following:

John scored at the 80th percentile on the 100-item final exam in history given to his class of fifty students. This means that John

a. Answered eighty items correctly
b. Scored higher than forty students in the class
c. Scored lower than forty students in the class
d. Scored 80 percent higher than the average student

This item measures at a higher cognitive level because it requires the student to interpret the meaning of a percentile.

Another source of items is the students themselves. Instructors can have each student write four or five multiple-choice questions over the content. Many of these will be low-level questions, but even if instructors get only a few usable items, it will be a worthwhile pedagogical exercise for the students. Writing items will help students learn the material, and getting involved in this way may lower student anxiety about the test. At the least, students will probably gain an appreciation of the difficulty of writing multiple-choice items.

Buchanan and Rogers (1990) report on their success in using student-generated test items. Before the first exam, they suggest that students submit up to ten multiple-choice questions in a specified format (typed on a five-by-seven card with the correct answer and its source given). Students are motivated to write items because they can see their own questions on the test (with their names attached if they wish) and they receive two extra points for each of their questions used. No more than two questions from any student are ever used on a single test. Buchanan and Rogers find that each student on the average submits from one to one and one half questions per test; this results in a very large number of potential test items in their large classes. They go through the items, sort the promising ones into categories that fit the table of specifications, and discard the rest. From among the good items, a lottery approach is used to draw the right number for the test. Although they find that many of the items require some rewriting, they are generally satisfied with the items' quality and with this procedure for constructing a multiple-choice test.

The Use of Multiple-Choice Items

We illustrate the versatility of the multiple-choice format by providing sample items from a number of different disciplines. We have not attempted to classify the items according to levels of Bloom's taxonomy, but we can see that most of them measure complex cognitive skills rather than simple factual knowledge. Perhaps these items may serve as models for developing multiple-choice questions that test higher-level objectives.

Economics

1. "A paradox occurred last year in the housing market. A study showed that the average price of new homes increased 7.5 percent to $104,100 but more new homes were sold." The best explanation for the above "paradox" is a(an)

a.   Outward shift in the demand curve for homes
b.   Movement by home buyers along their demand curves for homes
c.   Decrease in supply of homes (higher asking prices for homes by contractors due to higher costs of production)
d.   Perfectly inelastic demand for homes, so that buyers must pay higher asking prices for homes because they have no alternatives

2. In describing the pricing policy for its retail stores, the J.C. Penney company once stated: "Merchandise was sold at the lowest prices possible, on the theory that many sales at low profit were better than few sales at high profit." As described in this statement, J.C. Penney can be called a firm in

a.   "Perfect competition" operating on the elastic portion of its demand curve
b.   "Perfect competition" operating on the inelastic portion of its demand curve
c.   "Imperfect competition" operating on the elastic portion of its demand curve

d.   "Imperfect competition" operating on the inelastic portion of its demand curve

3. The Federal Reserve has sometimes been criticized for not increasing the nation's money supply fast enough. If the Federal Reserve feels that the money supply should be increased faster, it might

a.   Raise the discount rate and buy bonds in the open market
b.   Raise the discount rate and sell bonds in the open market
c.   Lower the discount rate and buy bonds in the open market
d.   Lower the discount rate and sell bonds in the open market

4. "Consumers' eagerness to buy durable goods, such as cars and houses, in advance of expected price increases has resulted in an increase in interest rates because those items frequently require financing." It follows from this statement that:

I.   Inflationary expectations increase the demand for loanable funds.
II. Bond prices will be driven up by consumers trying to borrow money to finance purchases.

a.   I only
b.   II only
c.   Both I and II
d.   Neither I nor II

Biology

1. Carbon monoxide (CO) is a "cell poison" that affects various enzymes of the cytochrome system (of terminal respiration). If CO is added to a sealed aquarium, which organism is most likely to survive? (Assume that CO is soluble in water.)

a.   Anaerobic bacteria living in the mud
b.   *Elodea* (a green plant)

c. Green pond scum
d. Small animals called rotifers
e. Snails that can come up for air

2. Suppose you thoroughly and adequately examined a particular type of cell, using the transmission electron microscope, and discovered that it completely lacked ribosomes. You could then conclude that this cell type also *lacked*

a. A nucleus
b. DNA
c. Cellulose
d. Protein synthesis

3. Some viruses have RNA but no DNA. This would indicate that

a. These viruses cannot replicate
b. These viruses have no heritable information.
c. RNA can act to transmit hereditary information of these viruses.
d. Their nucleic acids must combine with host DNA for virus replication.
e. They can direct the manufacture of proteins but not of nucleic acids.

4. Phenylketonuria (PKU) is an autosomal recessive condition. About one in every fifty individuals is heterozygous for the gene but shows no symptoms of the disorder. If you select a *symptom-free* male and a *symptom-free* female at random, what is the probability that they could have a child afflicted with PKU?

a. $(.02)(.02)(.25) = 0.0001 = .01\%$, or about 1/10,000
b. $(.02)(.02) = 0.0004 = .04\%$, or about 1/2,500
c. $(1)(50)(0) = 0 = $ none
d. $1/50 = .02 = 2\%$, or 2/100
e. $(1)(50)(2) = 100\% = $ all

Business Law

1. Julian D. Hursey, Jr., was convicted of violating a Daytona Beach, Florida, ordinance prohibiting "public night-napping." Mr. Hursey weighs 375 pounds and suffers from Pickwickian syndrome, a disease that affects overweight persons by reducing oxygen intake, thereby causing them to fall asleep. Mr. Hursey was arrested for being asleep in his pickup truck at 2:00 A.M. while the truck was parked on a public street. Mr. Hursey's best argument for getting his conviction overturned on appeal would be that

a. The State of Florida cannot make this conduct a crime because it is constitutionally protected behavior.
b. The ordinance is "void for vagueness."
c. He did not have the capacity to form the required *mens rea* for this crime.
d. The ordinance is being applied to him as an ex post facto law.

2. Assume now that Mr. Hursey claims at trial and on appeal that the night-napping ordinance violated the U.S. Constitution but that the Florida Supreme Court affirmed both the constitutionality of the ordinance and his conviction. What can Hursey do if he still wants to appeal?

a. He has only one option left — to petition the U.S. Supreme Court for a writ of certiorari and hope that the Court decides to consider his appeal.
b. He has no right to appeal further because he was convicted under a Florida ordinance and his conviction was affirmed by the highest court of that state.
c. He can compel the U.S. Supreme Court to review his conviction under its appeal jurisdiction; the Court must consider his appeal.
d. He cannot appeal his conviction to any federal court because he has not raised any "federal question."

3. In November of 1988, John Smith was served the equivalent of six quarts of beer over a period of about three hours. The bartender knew that Smith was intoxicated but continued to serve him. When Smith drove home, his car struck a car driven by Ronald Hill, severely injuring Hill, his wife, and child. Because Smith had no money, Hill sued the bartender. Hill will

a. Lose because Smith is the only proper defendant in this case
b. Win on a theory of negligence per se
c. Lose because the bartender is not liable for the conduct of Smith, a third-party customer of the pub
d. Win on a theory of *res ipsa loquitur*

4. James Riggs answered an ad in *Soldier of Fortune* magazine that promised $10,000 to men willing to participate in a mercenary mission. He traveled to Anderson, Indiana, where he and eight other men were arrested in an Anderson motel room and charged with conspiring to storm a Madison County courtroom and help a convicted murderer escape. Riggs was acquitted of the conspiracy charge, but six months later filed notice that he planned to sue for $300,000 in damages. Which intentional tort(s) could Riggs possibly prove?

a. Wrongful civil process only
b. Malicious prosecution only
c. Malicious prosecution and abuse of process
d. Abuse of process and wrongful civil process

Journalism

1. Some media researchers and political scientists (specifically, the Survey Research Center at the University of Michigan) are concerned with the contemporary role of media in political affairs because

a. The large corporations that now own many media news sources will be able to conspire to pick candidates and even select presidents.

b. Election returns in the eastern states may have an impact on voting behavior in the western states.

c. Personality factors may be more important than issues.

d. Media concentration means less information in the "marketplace of ideas."

e. Segmentation strategies will ultimately mean that each individual bases his or her decision on a different set of facts.

2. Dominick explained that the Arbitron and Nielson ratings are less than ideal for a variety of reasons. Which reason was *not* among those included?

a. The minuscule sample size compared to the overall population biases the results in favor of those who participated in the survey.

b. People who agree to participate may have different viewing habits than people who decline.

c. People who return questionnaires may be different from those who do not return the questionnaires.

d. Minorities, the poor, the elderly, and those with minimal education tend to be underrepresented.

e. Stations may bias the results by presenting the programs they expect will generate the greatest viewership during sweeps periods.

3. According to DeFleur, the ownership by one person or company of both print and broadcasting outlets is called

a. Longitudinal ownership
b. Cross-media ownership
c. Group or chain ownership
d. Media monopoly
e. Media partnership

4. According to the 1984 FCC rules that limit ownership of broadcast properties, an owner can have

a. Up to twelve TV, twelve AM radio, and twelve FM stations
b. Up to seven TV, seven AM, and seven FM stations

c. An unlimited number of stations as long as a single owner does not reach more than 25 percent of the total population

d. Twelve television stations and up to twelve radio stations in any combination

e. As many as twenty-one broadcast properties in any combination as long as the owner does not reach more than 25 percent of the total population

Political Science

1. Yugoslavia is currently beset with ethnic strife. The ability of the country to maintain cohesion in the early decades after World War II is largely attributable to the charisma of the wartime hero

a. Konrad Adenauer
b. Trygve Lie
c. Thomas Masaryk
d. Marshal Tito

2. Before being named U.S. ambassador to the U.N., Jeanne Kirkpatrick had gained recognition among neoconservatives for writings in which she

a. Distinguished between the necessity under some circumstances of providing U.S. aid to authoritarian regimes and the unacceptability under any circumstances of normal relations with totalitarian regimes

b. Expressed support for the Carter human rights program

c. Explained why a conciliatory policy with Castro's Cuba was likely to prove far more successful in reducing Soviet influence in the region than the current hard-line approach

d. Provided a convincing argument for the Nixon-Kissinger policies of détente with the Soviet Union

3. As director of the CIA under President Reagan, William Casey helped to organize U.S. support for

a. Castro
b. Contras
c. PLO
d. Sandinistas

4. According to the lecture, the West German "Ostpolitik" initiative is credited to

a. Helmut Kohl
b. Willy Brandt
c. Helmut Schmidt
d. Karl von Clausewitz

Music

Use the following musical passage to answer questions 1–3.

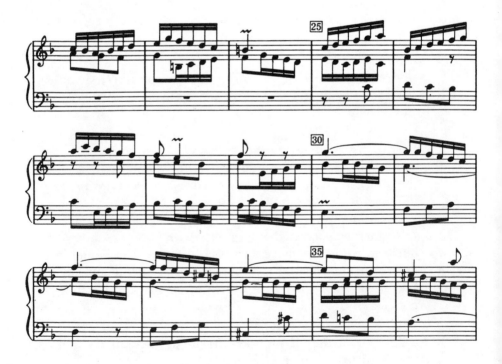

1. An instance of invertible counterpoint at the octave may be found if we compare which of the following?

a. Top and bottom voices meas. 27, with middle and bottom voices meas. 29
b. Top and middle voices meas. 22, with top and bottom voices meas. 26
c. Top and middle voices meas. 28, with top and bottom voices meas. 35
d. There is no instance of invertible counterpoint in the passage shown

2. The *top voice* in measures 30–34 illustrates

a. Hemiola
b. Interval contraction
c. Oblique motion
d. Parallel motion
e. Sequence and step progression

3. The harmonic progression (one chord per measure) in measures 34, 35, and 36 may best be described as

a. G minor: iv°7 ii 7 II7
b. D minor: V$^6_5$ i V
c. F major: #V IV7 V7/vi
d. C major: I II III
e. C minor: IV iii V

4. The humor in the last movement of Haydn's "Joke" string quartet (op. 33, no. 3) comes from which of the following effects?

a. A loud chord
b. Electronic effects
c. Pauses in the theme
d. Rapid scales suggesting drunkenness
e. Rapidly repeated notes suggesting foot stamping

5. A baroque form for voices and instrumental accompaniment, sometimes incorporating a chorale in one or more of the movements, is called a

a. Cantata
b. Madrigal
c. Mass
d. Motet
e. French overture

Geography

1. If you were digging on a soil pit in the midlatitude desert and encountered a clay pan, your interpretation might be that

a. The soil is very young.
b. The pan may be relict from a time of warmer, drier climate of the past.
c. The pan may be relict from a time of cooler, wetter climate of the past.
d. The pan suggests nothing unusual because such a feature should develop easily in a midlatitude desert environment.
e. The soil is burned often.

2. What channel form and sediment characteristics would you normally expect to characterize streams carrying glacial load?

a. Braided channel with coarse bed load
b. Braided channel with fine suspended load
c. Braided channel with dissolved load
d. Narrow deep channel with very little sediment load

3. Which one of the following features is the best example of a relict landform?

a. Frost-shattered rock in Wisconsin
b. Glacial moraines at the end of a present-day glacier in Alaska

c.   Masses of rock broken by frost shattering in Arctic Alaska
d.   Steep cliffs next to the North Atlantic

4. Why do you think there is little ozone in the middle tropo-
sphere compared to the upper stratosphere?

a.   There is little molecular oxygen.
b.   There is little atomic oxygen (O).
c.   There are few water molecules.
d.   There are too few collisions of molecules.

Summary

Multiple-choice tests can be used to measure a variety of content and learning objectives in the college classroom. Writing
good multiple-choice tests is a difficult and time-consuming task,
and instructors should start well ahead of time. Test items can
be accumulated and filed for access, but some new items should
be written for each test. Some sources for items are the instructor's manual that comes with the text and the students themselves.
     The following is a summary checklist for writing mul-
tiple-choice items:

1.   Make sure the item measures significant concepts and prin-
     ciples; do not write items covering trivia.
2.   The stem should present a problem; thus, a verb is neces-
     sary in the statement.
3.   State the item clearly and concisely and include only rele-
     vant material.
4.   Include as much of the item material as possible in the stem;
     do not repeat words or phrases in each distractor that could
     be put in the stem one time.
5.   Write one correct or clearly best answer and three or four
     plausible distractors.
6.   Avoid giving clues to the right answer; some common clues
     are grammatical, some involve length of the options, and
     some use specific determiners.

7. Use positively stated stems if possible; otherwise, call the students' attention to the negative.

8. Use "all of the above" and "none of the above" only rarely, and use "none of the above" only in the correct answer format.

9. Place the correct answer in each of the alternative positions approximately an equal number of times but in a random order.

5

True-False, Matching, and Completion Items

In this chapter, we discuss the construction and application of true-false, matching, and short-answer (or completion) items. It is our intent not only to help instructors become more versatile test writers but to do this in the context of creating tests that tap cognitive abilities at the higher levels of Bloom's taxonomy.

Writing effective items is essential to obtaining test validity. Not only must the items cover the topics and levels of cognitive functions in the table of specifications but they must also appropriately focus on the topics in such a way as to test the skills the students have developed. Because the length of tests are under some time restraint — usually one class period — instructors may need a variety of items with which to measure all outcomes efficiently.

True-False Items

The true-false item is essentially a declarative statement that the test-taker must decide is correct (true) or incorrect (false). Here is an example:

> T F The transcontinental railroad was completed before the discovery of gold at Sutter's mill in California.

The student reads the item and decides whether it is true or false. This type of item has been used widely because instructors can rapidly compose items of modest quality and can score the tests quickly and objectively. Well-written items initially take a little longer to construct but can be scored just as quickly.

Advantages and Disadvantages of True-False Items

There are some definite advantages to using true-false items. First, in a given time period, a true-false test can sample many more bits of information about a topic than any other type of test format. A typical class of college students can complete three true-false items in the same time they would complete two multiple-choice items (Frisbie, 1974). Consequently, if, during a class period, an instructor is able to sample forty features of course content with a multiple-choice test, he or she could sample sixty features with a true-false examination — a considerably larger sample of student performance.

True-false tests are believed to be easier to construct than some other types of tests. However, in writing true-false tests, a number of problems arise whose solutions are essential to test credibility. For example, it is often hard to avoid ambiguous statements without making the items obvious. Writing clearly true or clearly false items, without exceptions, is also a problem. Nevertheless, as one develops skill in the construction of true-false items, the job goes faster than writing a set of any other type of test items that covers the same breadth of topics.

True-false tests have a distinct limitation, however. Guessing is a big problem. On average, students will be correct on half of the items on which they guess. If a student knows half of the content and guesses at the other half, the score for this person, on average, should be 75 percent. Scoring formulas, originally devised to compensate for guessing, are often presented as a solution to this problem. The familiar formula for true-false tests is

$$\text{Score} = \text{Rights} - \text{Wrongs}$$

For example, on a fifty-item test, Mrs. Ecks got thirty-eight correct, missed ten, and left two blank. Her corrected score would be 38 – 10, or 28 (if the student does not know an item and leaves it blank, no penalty is assessed). This score of 23 assumes that items were missed because Mrs. Ecks did not know the answer and guessed. Since guessing correctly is a 50 percent chance in true-false tests, for every item Mrs. Ecks guessed at and got wrong, we can assume that she also guessed at one and got it right. That is, some of those right answers are presumed to have been marked correctly because of the probability of guessing. So Mrs. Ecks, who missed ten items, should have also guessed at ten others and got them correct. As a result, Mrs. Ecks's score is decreased by ten.

At first glance, this formula appears to be a means of either discouraging students from guessing or appropriately penalizing the rampant guessers. However, there are some definite flaws with the procedure. First, it assumes that all guessing is strictly random, an assumption that is probably not true. Most guessing is based on some logic or on partial knowledge, which allows a student to make an "educated guess" and improves the student's chances over random odds. Instructions to guess generally increase a student's score over instructions not to guess (Michael, Stewart, Douglass, and Rainwater, 1963). Apparently, students fall back on partial knowledge and on clues in the item context to jog their memories, a scheme that appears to improve their guessing over mere fifty-fifty chance.

Second, students are not all equally disposed to guessing. Some students will mark every item, even when told not to guess; others will leave a number of items blank. The scoring formula assumes that all students who do not know an item will leave it blank if told to do so in the test instructions. This is simply not the way all students respond to a test. Test-wise students, and bold personalities, will guess at every item they do not know. Recent research suggests that there may also be gender differences in the tendency to guess (Ben-Shakhar and Sinai, 1991). Consequently, scores with which we rank our students on achievement of course objectives do not reflect knowledge of the topic alone but are contaminated with students' gender differences and character traits.

To deal with a part of this problem when giving a true-false test, instructors should advise students to respond to every item. Scoring formulas may be used to sort out the wild guessers, but if instructions are given to attempt every item, the ranking of students will be essentially the same whether the formula is used or not. It is, therefore, our recommendation that instructors not use the scoring formula on classroom tests.

Guessing can seriously affect the reliability and validity of true-false tests. Here is an example. Steve knows the answer to six of the items in a ten-item test (the test is too short but works fine for the example). He does not guess at the other four items. Carla also knows six answers, but she guesses at the other four and, doing so on a random basis, may get two more right, making her score 8. The results are tabulated below:

Test taker	Items known	Guessed	Total
Steve	6	0	6
Carla	6	2	8

When we use tests we are trying to rank students on what they know about the unit of instruction. In this example, we have two people who "know" the same amount, but Carla, a bold guesser, is two points higher than Steve, who does not guess. This is a validity problem. Our test has not ranked students entirely on what they know about the course content laid out in the table of specifications for the unit of instruction. Instructors can in large part deal with this problem if students are told to attempt every item in the test. If Steve guesses, we would expect both students to be ranked at about the same place in the score range.

We may wish to think of Carla's 2-point advantage as measurement error and hence a factor in test reliability. The data indeed show that true-false tests are less reliable than multiple-choice tests (Ebel, 1975). However, since an instructor can administer more true-false items in a single class period than multiple-choice items, test writers can partially compensate for this slightly lower reliability by increasing the test length (which we saw in Chapter Three is expected to increase reliability). Therefore, the reliability difference is not a serious problem in choosing between the two test types, especially if the tests are reasonably long ones.

All considered, it appears that the true-false test is sufficiently reliable and valid for at least periodic use in classroom testing. This is especially true when we consider the fact that true-false tests can sample up to a third more items of content. However, adequate sampling depends on skill in writing the items in true-false tests. And the basics of this skill constitute the next topic we explore.

Writing True-False Test Items

The quality of true-false tests can be improved considerably if a few rules are followed in writing the test items. Here are the features to keep in mind while writing these items.

1. Avoid the use of specific determiners. These are words that serve as special clues to the answer by presenting conditions as absolute or as qualified. When an item includes absolute terms such as *all* or *always,* it probably is false. There are exceptions, of course, but test takers play the probabilities, and only occasionally does something *always* happen.

A second class of specific determiners is made up of qualifying terms such as a *sometimes, usually, typically.* These qualifiers have a very uncertain definition and suggest that the item is true.

Here are some examples of specific determiners that illustrate how absolutes reflect "false," while qualifiers reflect "true."

1. Mercury is *always* in a liquid state. (absolute)
2. Plants *usually* require sunlight for normal growth. (qualifier)
3. *All* broad leafed plants are deciduous. (absolute)
4. Rembrandt *typically* painted portraits. (qualifier)

In the first item, it is a safe bet to guess false, because many elements change their state from liquid to solid with temperature and pressure changes. In the second item, the test writer presents a proposition but admits there are exceptions. To many test takers, an exception characterizes a true statement, and they will often be correct.

In the third example, *all* is the clue; betting on an exception to every rule, the student should mark the item false. And in the fourth example, some students will be familiar with Rembrandt's portraits but not his other work; however, since the item provides for exceptions by saying "typically," it is a safe guess that the item is true. By having just a little bit of knowledge and by following the specific determiners, students can get a number of items correct without knowing all the details of a subject.

2. Avoid the use of indefinite terms denoting degree or amount:

> T F   A long time ago trees covered a very
> large part of present-day Wyoming.

What does "a long time ago" mean? Under the ground in Wyoming are hundreds of thousands of tons of fossilized fuel (coal and oil) that must have come from vegetation, so if the instructor means thousands of years ago, then the item could be true. But to the student reading the item, "a long time ago" could mean in 1850; in this case the item is probably false, since much of eastern and southern Wyoming has been relatively treeless for hundreds of years. In this item, we also will puzzle over the meaning of "a very large part."

Indefinite words and phrases tend to make items ambiguous, and, consequently, they open up the answer to vigorous discussion when the test is returned to students. Unfortunately, these terms change their meaning depending on context. They may also mean different things to different age groups. For example, most elderly would agree that the Civil War was fought "a long time ago," but most adolescents would think World War II was fought "a long time ago." The phrase has little specific meaning, and hence its meaning is arguable. If these terms or phrases seem appropriate to writers of a true-false test, they should give some objective reference for the reader to use in judging the term's meaning. Here is an example:

>   *Poor:* In his study of AIDS, Dr. Wye found
> that many of those who contracted the HIV virus
> were exposed through use of drug needles that had
> been used by an infected person.
>   *Better:* In his study of AIDS, Dr. Wye found
> that many (over 20 percent) of those who contracted
> the HIV virus . . .

In the revision of the item, we have given a specific definition for the term *many,* which makes the item more objective.

3. True-false items should be positive, declarative sentences, stated as simply as possible. Negative statements should be avoided. Instructors are trying to assess students' knowledge of a topical area, not their skill in reading and interpreting complex sentences.

However, complex sentences can be used without making them so convoluted that their meaning is obscure. For example, occasionally instructors will want to use compound sentences in which they first lay out a condition, followed by an explanation. Much information, and application of information, is conditional; the appropriateness of an action depends on the condition in which it is imposed. The condition should be true, but the explanation may or may not be true. Consider the following example:

> Because the combustion of gasoline creates gases
> that pollute the air, cars produce more pollutants
> at fifty miles per hour than at thirty miles per hour.

In this item, the condition in the initial clause is true, as it should be, and the student must decide if the second clause is true or false. Items using this format tend to be straightforward and focused in their presentation of information on a specific issue. Therefore, later discussions between instructor and students about the point of a question can generally be avoided. This format also produces items that test the higher levels of cognitive demand. Application, synthesis, and so on can best be tested by first presenting a setting for a problem, then presenting a "solution" that may be correct or incorrect.

4. To make administering and scoring of true-false tests easier, the directions should clearly indicate the method students should use in reporting their answers. If the tests are to be hand-scored, here are some tips to improve directions. Never ask students to use plus for true and minus for false. The minuses are too easy to change to pluses after the test is returned. If symbols are used, have students use plus and zero. The safest procedure is to have students write out "true" and "false" for their responses. Or instructors can print *T* and *F* in the left-hand margin next to the item number and have students circle their choice. Some instructors find this method faster to score than the "write-out" method.

Application of the True-False Test

True-false tests are sometimes criticized because so many users limit their use to the lower levels of Bloom's taxonomy. Indeed, it is easier to write an item at a strictly factual level than at the so called higher levels such as evaluation or analysis. It is the purpose of this section, therefore, to lay out some procedures for writing true-false items at more complex cognitive levels. Consider the following example:

> T F   In "To a Mountain Daisy," Burns's point
>   is that lives are often snuffed out without
>   being recognized.

In this item, the student must think at an abstract level, integrate the parts of the poem, and reach the generalization across the entire poem. Here is another example:

> In *Hamlet,* Shakespeare says,
> "No; let candied tongues lick absurd pomp
> And crook the pregnant hinges of the knee
> Where thrift may follow fauning."
>
> T F   Shakespeare means that one should not hasten
>   to cater to one's own weaknesses.

In this example, the student must analyze the expression to get its meaning, based on translation of the vernacular. This question reaches above mere repetition of factual content.

Here is an example in the field of social psychology:

Students were required to wear uniforms to grade school. After three months, the requirement was removed, but the majority of the students continued to wear their uniforms.

T F   This is an example of psychic inertia.

Here the student must understand the concept of psychic inertia and then analyze the situation to see if it falls within the concept. Again, the item presents demands above the repetition of mere facts.

The use of propositional logic is one approach to getting at higher cognitive levels with true-false tests. Using the "if-then" approach, instructors can present a hypothetical situation and ask a question about what will follow. First lay out a proposition or a brief paragraph describing a situation. Then ask students either what would be the impact on a related event or, given the situation, what would happen if a certain element were changed. Here is an example:

Under the current money policy of the Federal Reserve Bank, the prime rate is .09 and the inflation rate is .04. The gross national product is down .03, and the unemployment rate is 7 percent. A slowdown of the economy is taking place.

T F   If the Federal Reserve reduces the prime rate, the inflation rate is expected to rise.

T F   If the gross national product goes up and the other indicators stay the same, the Dow Jones averages will probably respond by going up.

More complex situations are desirable because they will provide the possibility for writing several items for each situation, but the above example illustrates the procedure. Here the student must have some understanding of the relation between the availability of money and the inflation rate. The student must apply this knowledge to solving the problem and do some analysis of the data to conclude how an indicator like gross national product affects the market. This process requires not just knowledge but the ability to analyze situations and apply the knowledge to solutions of problems.

Another approach to creating more challenging true-false items is to ask students to look at a problem, analyze it, and identify solutions. Again we provide a short description of a problem and ask questions about it. Here is an example of this procedure, maybe a little obvious, but illustrative:

> Last night John bought a used car. This morning it would not start. John begins to search for the possible *causes of the car's failure to start*. Decide whether each statement is or is not a plausible reason for the car not starting.
>
> T F   The carburetor may be malfunctioning.
> T F   The exhaust manifold may be loose.
> T F   The battery may be discharged.
> T F   The car may be out of gasoline.

Asking students to sort out the relevant and irrelevant requires them to analyze and synthesize data and to evaluate alternatives — our objective in assessing higher-order cognitive operations. These illustrations show that true-false items can surely deal with mental operations other than recall of simple facts. Within the context of your own discipline, first try some examples that correspond with the above examples. Very soon you will discover that your skill in writing true-false items will take you into ever more imaginative application of this test technique at the upper levels of Bloom's categories.

Multiple True-False Items

A variation of the true-false item is the multiple true-false test. This type contains a stem followed by a number of statements, each one being either true or false in regard to the stem. Here is an example:

The Boston Tea Party (1773) was

_____ a. Actually carried out by Indians
_____ b. Planned as a revolt against taxes
_____ c. Done because the tea market in America was
overstocked and prices were falling

Each response describes — accurately or inaccurately — the Boston Tea Party. With this type of item, we can ask a number of questions about a single topic, making our test more diagnostic. This advantage, however, is also a limitation. We saw that one advantage of the true-false test was its ability to sample a wide range of topics in a relatively short time. Since we concentrate a little more time on each topic with multiple true-false items, we will have less time to add more topics to the test.

Multiple true-false items are a middle ground between multiple-choice and true-false items. Simply finding a response that is true is adequate for multiple-choice items, but in the multiple true-false item, any or all of the alternatives could be true, or false, a fact that forces the student to regard the aspects of each option very carefully. Nevertheless, in a given time period, students can do more items of multiple true-false than they can multiple-choice. Further, there is evidence (Frisbie and Sweeney, 1982) that students generally prefer multiple true-false tests to multiple-choice items and find them less difficult.

There is also evidence that these tests are more reliable than multiple-choice tests, possibly because they include more scored items, thus spreading out the score range. There is a practical problem with multiple true-false tests that should be mentioned. Not all scoring machines can readily score items with more than one right answer. This is an inconvenience but should not be regarded as a reason to totally avoid a test technique. One solution to this problem is to number the alternatives consecutively through the test. Students would then mark the answer sheet just as they would with a true-false test.

The rules for developing the multiple true-false item are the same as those for the standard true-false item (a review of these will improve the writing of the multiple true-false as well as the standard true-false item). A couple of additional points should be mentioned in regard to multiple true-false items. The number of true alternatives for an item can vary from none to all, and care should be taken to avoid a pattern of any kind in the order or number of correct alternatives. Additionally, the number of alternatives can vary from item to item. Because each alternative in multiple true-false tests is in fact a separate test item, we can have four options for one item, six for another, and three for another. This practice is not recommended for the multiple-choice test, where item difficulty is to some extent dependent on the number of alternatives provided for the item.

Here are some examples of multiple true-false items from several disciplines. Each is intended to test at a higher level than knowledge on the Bloom taxonomy.

Science. A large glass is turned upside down over a small potted plant whose soil has been covered over with plastic. The next day the inside of the glass has small water droplets on it. From this demonstration we can rightly conclude that

_____ a. The water droplets are from the plant's transpiration.
_____ b. Without a control (an inverted glass without a plant), we cannot conclude where the water came from.
_____ c. The water came from the humidity already existing in the air before the plant was enclosed.

Literature. In *Wuthering Heights,* Heathcliff may be characterized as

_____ a. Distant
_____ b. Warmhearted
_____ c. Brooding
_____ d. Pedantic

Social Studies. Suppose the Lowndes-Calhoun tariff of 1816 had not been enacted. What effect would this have had on American industry and commerce?

_____ a. American industry would have become more com-
petitive.
_____ b. The tonnage of foreign imports would have
decreased.

The above examples are intended to be illustrative of items
that will tap higher mental operations. Our intent in providing
these examples is to show that true-false and multiple true-false
items need not deal with basic factual material. We believe that
knowledge of facts is the foundation for reasoning, but we value
higher mental functions as an essential outcome of education.
We hope that the above suggestions will be employed extensively among faculty in making up their true-false tests.

Short-Answer or Completion Items

The typical completion item is a statement missing key words
that the student must fill in. In the short-answer item, the student is asked a specific question that requires a response of only
a few words. Here are examples of both.

Completion: There are _____ members of the U.S. House of
Representatives and _____ members of the Senate.
Short answer: How many members are there in the U.S.
House of Representatives and how many in the Senate?

In completion and short-answer tests, the student gets
minimal cues and must construct the answer, while in multiple-
choice tests, the student must only recognize the correct response
among the responses given. Many test makers like to use completion items because they believe the demand on the student
is greater due to the items' demand for recall of information,
not recognition.

Whether or not this argument is true, there are situations
where the completion and short-answer tests are useful, and,
for this reason, we look at how to do a competent job of constructing them. However, they do not assess higher cognitive
levels well. They are best used to see how well students have
collected basic information pertinent to the course.

The authors once saw an item from a health science test that read, "A chemical poisoning is _____ ." The intended answer was "ptomaine," but we and many students saw other plausible answers. This is clearly a poorly constructed item. Here are some rules that will help instructors avoid problems in constructing completion and short-answer items.

1. If at all possible, write completion items that can be answered with a single word. This takes the subjectivity out of scoring and also makes scoring faster to complete. For example, consider the following items:

> The density of a fluid is measured with an instrument called the _____ .
> The hydrometer is used to measure _____ .

In the first item, a single word correctly answers the item. In the second item, because several words are required, students will write different answers, encouraging instructors to give only partial credit to students who word their answers awkwardly.

2. Statements should be worded so that they have only one right answer. For example:

> The battle of Lexington was fought in _____ .

This statement can be answered by several "right" answers. Students could list the state, the year, the season of the year, the war, and so on, all of which would be correct but probably not all of which would get credit from the instructor. Indefinite statements lead only to controversy when students get their papers back. The above item could be better written as:

> The battle of Lexington was fought in the year _____ .

3. Delete only key words from statements. Instructors are after the student's knowledge of the important, and central, aspects of a concept, and their items should reflect that intent.

4. Do not lift statements directly from the textbook for completion or short-answer items. This encourages students to memorize, not understand, the readings for the course.

5. Make all blanks the same length so that they do not provide a clue to the length of the answer.

Although scoring of completion items has been adapted to machine-scorable answer sheets, it is laborious and subject to random errors. Consequently, we do not generally recommend it. Instead, the test sheet can be written as in Exhibit 5.1.

**Exhibit 5.1. A Layout to
Facilitate Scoring of Completion-Type Tests.**

The quality of a test that deals with consistency
is called (1), and the quality that deals with the   1. _____
extent to which a test relates to a criterion is
called (2).   2. _____

Here the items are listed on the left, with the blanks numbered. The student writes the answer in the blank at the right that corresponds with the number in the text on the left. This greatly facilitates scoring. The example in Exhibit 5.1 works well for the completion test but does not fit the short-answer format well, because the response space is small.

To summarize, completion and short-answer tests have some real advantages. They depend on recall, not recognition, they are applicable to almost all kinds of topics, they can be scored relatively easily, and they also put variety into tests. They are worth incorporating into instructors' test kits.

The Matching Item

Long used in public schools to measure simple associations, the matching test has not been widely used in colleges and universities. However, there are indeed topics in which matching tests can quickly assess achievement across a fairly wide content domain.

The matching test is characterized by two columns of topics. The left column contains the stimuli — a list of terms — that will be matched with the responses — a second list of terms or descriptions. Here is an example:

In the space beside each battle listed on the left, put the letter of the state given on the right in which the battle was fought.

_____ 1. Andersonville   a. Mississippi
_____ 2. Antietam   b. Maryland
_____ 3. Bull Run   c. Tennessee
_____ 4. Perryville   d. Georgia
_____ 5. Shiloh   e. Virginia
_____ 6. Vicksburg   f. Kentucky
                                 g. Pennsylvania

Although associative learning is the focus of matching tests, it is also possible to adapt the test to the application and higher levels of Bloom's taxonomy. Later in the chapter, we provide an example of the use of matching at the higher cognitive level.

Guidelines for Writing Matching Items

If matching items are to be reliable and valid, they must be constructed according to certain specifications. The following are some rules that may help instructors write better matching tests.

1. To cut down on random error from accidental markings, place the stimulus column on the left, with each item numbered, and the response column on the right, with the items lettered. There should be more responses than there are stimuli so that the last choice requires a decision, too.

2. Provide marking spaces for students to write their responses to the left of the stimuli. Written instructions should be provided at the top of the exercise.

3. Each matching exercise should contain only homogeneous material. If an exercise has phyla for stimuli and responses made up of animals to be sorted into these phyla, then it should not also include genus or species stimuli with animals to be sorted into these categories, too. A separate exercise should be made for each type of content. There is a very good reason for this—

heterogeneous material makes the test easier. Here is a short but illustrative example:

_____ 1. George Washington   a. A Revolutionary War general

_____ 2. John Hancock   b. One of the original colonies

_____ 3. Virginia   c. A signer of the Declaration of Independence

    Only one stimulus is a state, so we can quickly sort out the response most appropriate for a state, whether or not we know that Virginia was one of the original colonies. Anytime the test taker can cut down the options from which the response is to be made, the test gets easier. And including more than one topic in a test sets up such a situation.

    4. The test-taking task is simpler if we arrange items in a systematic order of some type. Alphabetizing the stimuli is one way of doing this; putting events into chronological order is another. These procedures are done simply to make the job of taking the test easier, so that students can concentrate on the content instead of being distracted by hunting for topics.

    5. Matching tests should not be too short or too long. The minimum length for college students should be about ten stimuli, but the test probably should not exceed fifteen.

    6. The entire test should be on a single page so that students do not have to shift back and forth across pages to find matches. This paging back and forth increases the chances for students to make errors in marking the intended response.

Matching and Higher-Level Cognitive Demands

As noted earlier, the matching test is often thought to measure only simple associations, a skill that is usually classified on the Bloom taxonomy as knowledge. However, it can be used to test higher-level cognitive objectives, if we put our minds to it. Below is an example of such a matching test. The stimulus column lists a set of simple machines, and the response column lists applications. The student will select the application that is an example of the machine.

Machine	*Example*
____ 1. Inclined plane	a. Operating a pump handle
____ 2. Lever	b. Cutting with an ax
____ 3. Pulley	c. Lifting a cargo onto a ship with block and tackle
____ 4. Screw	d. Rolling a hoop along a street
____ 5. Wedge	e. Sliding a box down the tail gate of a truck
	f. Drilling a hole with a bit auger

And here is an example from a different discipline. The student is to match the opera with a generalization from its plot.

Opera	*Generalization*
____ 1. "The Bartered Bride"	a. The spell of evil can be broken.
____ 2. "Carmen"	b. Rewards of art are consolation for a broken heart.
____ 3. "Tales of Hoffman"	c. Bearing many trials is the path to true love.
____ 4. "Lohengrin"	d. Scheming women can get what they set out to get.
____ 5. "The Magic Flute"	e. Little sins pile up to bigger and bigger ones.
	f. The solution to most problems can be found in money.

Before we leave the matching test, we should note that there are ten-option answer sheets available from some electronic-scoring services. These answer sheets can be adapted to use with matching exercises as long as there are no more than nine matches (ten response options, nine stimuli). Also, companies that print test answer sheets will be happy to custom design one, but unless many of them are to be used, the designing costs are too great.

Summary

In this chapter, we have pointed out a variety of test item types with which to assess student achievement of instructional objectives. These optional item types can be written to measure at higher cognitive levels (our intent is not to downgrade the need for factual content but to point out the need to measure higher levels of cognitive demand). We have presented here four types of objectively scored items as alternatives to the multiple-choice tests presented earlier. These are the true-false, multiple true-false, short-answer and completion, and matching tests. The versatility of these items may not be as great as that of multiple-choice test items, but they provide variety for the test taker and definitely have application to assessing the achievement of instructional objectives in certain areas. We highly recommend use of these test types, not only as alternatives to other test types but also in conjunction with them.

6

Essay Examinations

Many faculty prefer to use essay tests because they believe that essays convey thinking processes, whereas objective tests do not. Faculty feel that students with orderly writing styles, who present clear propositions and support them with logic and references, think in a similarly orderly manner. It is proposed by some faculty that the written treatise provides access to the student's rational processes in a way that could never be matched by objective tests.

Essay test users often report that they see the multiple-choice test as prompting the student to think uncritically and in a probabilistic manner, and to accept selected propositions from a set of prompts. They believe the essay test provides no such prompting and does not point the student's response.

These opinions about essay testing, if true, support essays as an important assessment procedure. Essays may well provide that important access to students' mental operations. However, if essays are that powerful, at least a portion of the power depends on how clearly the instructor has posed the essay question and how carefully he or she has evaluated what the writer has said, in spite of how it was said. This is certainly not an easy task, because assessing the quality of a student's script is likely to be influenced by a variety of stimuli besides the rational quality of the essay. For this reason, much of our discussion deals with problems and procedures in scoring essay tests.

In this chapter, we first look at the advantages of essays, followed by some of the limitations. Then the validity of common student beliefs about essay tests is explored. Next some ideas to improve the essay test are suggested, followed by information on scoring and suggestions for improving the consistency, if not the burden, of scoring essay tests.

Advantages of Using Essay Examinations

Beyond the proposed features cited above, essay tests have several other specific advantages that make them attractive to many users. Essay tests (1) are most advantageous when assessing complex learning outcomes, (2) are relatively easy to construct, (3) emphasize communication skills as a fundamental performance in all areas of complex academic disciplines, (4) cannot be answered by simply recognizing the correct response, but require the student to construct the response, and (5) do not permit students to get a score by guessing (although they will bluff). Here is a more detailed look at these propositions.

Assessment of Higher-Level Skills

The main advantage of essay exams is that they provide a measure of the more complex learning outcomes. The higher-level cognitive skills that instructors focus on in their instructional objectives of a subject should be included in the assessment plan. In an earlier chapter, some procedures were described for using multiple-choice tests to assess these complex mental processes; however, essay tests have an important role here, too. In spite of the fact that well-made objective tests can get at problem-solving ability, analysis, and evaluation, they still depend on *recognition* of the correct answer. But essay tests require students to *recall* information, to perceive the necessary relationships, and to construct the answer, unaided. They enable instructors to see how students select, organize, and evaluate ideas and apply them to answering the questions. The essay should definitely be considered as one alternative in measuring student achievement of these complex cognitive outcomes. However, essays should not be used to get at basic factual matter, associative learning, and similar lower-level cognitive objectives. Here other types of tests are more efficient.

Ease of Test Construction

Somewhat easier to prepare than some objective tests, essay tests usually require only about four or five questions to fill a typical class period. The construction time for this many items will be less than that for, say, thirty-five to forty-five multiple-choice items.

However, essay test building can be deceptive in its time requirements. To create a good test, the instructor should sample a wide range of course objectives. The test should also be evaluated against a course blueprint such as Bloom's taxonomy (Chapter Two). Since only four or five items will be written to cover a fairly wide array of topics at several cognitive levels, the instructor must first think over the spread of topics and the range of cognitive functions that were intended to be developed in the instructional unit. Then the test questions can be written to sample and integrate these topics as well as focus on the appropriate levels of mental complexity. If this is done well, it may take somewhat more time than one would normally think necessary to write four or five test items.

Emphasis on Communication Skills

Essay tests require students to communicate their ideas in sentences and paragraphs, a skill that plays a large role in all fields of academic endeavor. Many teachers will indeed say that one objective of their instruction is to promote the student's ability to communicate the ideas presented in the course. If skill in communication is specifically promoted as an instructional objective, it should be assessed, but only if instructors have invested time in teaching students how to communicate within the course area. Instruction may include attention to unique vocabulary, relevant arguments for and against given points of view, and writing styles, such as formal scientific or open literary.

Control of Guessing

Students cannot guess on an essay test. If the range of options to a question is given, students can make an informed (sometimes not so informed) guess at which one is the correct option. But in essay tests no such set of options is given. They must deal with an array of possibilities, and without knowing which are the correct ones, must construct an answer. This is much more difficult than guessing one out of a group of five multiple choices.

However, they will do their best to make some kind of response, even if they do not know the details of a good answer. They will bluff rather than lose, say, 20 percent of the test's points. One student remarked, "I always put down as many things as I can think of that may be relevant, hoping to hit on something that will give me credit." Another supported this claim with, "You can make a pretty good essay if you know just a little bit of the answer, and I always do what I can with what I've got." To complicate matters, students, after having their papers returned to them with marks and comments, will see instructors after class to "explain" how their answer is relevant to the content of a "good" answer and will argue for a grade enhancement. In essay tests, there is no guessing in the classical sense, but bluffing occurs both during the writing and after the grading of the test.

Limitations of Essay Tests

All testing procedures have difficulties, and essay tests are no exception. In spite of their capability to reflect the thinking processes of students, essay tests have several limitations: (1) they are difficult to score, (2) their scores are less reliable than well-written objective tests, (3) they provide a very limited sample of the content in the typical unit of study, (4) their scores are influenced by the reader's overall impression of the student, and (5) they do not provide a good situation in which to develop good writing skills. Here is a look at each of these limitations in more detail.

Difficulty of Scoring

Scoring essays is tedious and time-consuming. The instructor goes through page after page of writing, some of it legible, some not so legible. Some essays are written in flawless grammar, and some with a wide variety of spelling and grammatical errors. Through all of this distraction, the reader tries to keep in mind a set of criteria to apply evenly across all papers. Does this describe your experience with the job of reading a set of essay tests?

Lower Reliability of Scores

The research evidence shows that the scores of essay tests are somewhat less reliable than the scores of objective tests. As early as 1913, Starch and Elliott, working in the more objective area of mathematics, showed that competent teachers cannot agree on what constitutes a correct answer on an essay test. In their studies, 116 teachers graded the same geometry paper and assigned scores ranging from 28 to 92 percent. Although skill in scoring essays has no doubt improved over the years, the general conclusion that two readers will not agree has been verified more recently by Van den Bergh and Eiting (1989).

To get a different view of score reliability, Ashburn (1938) showed that when college instructors read the same paper on two different occasions, their scores are likely to disagree from the first reading to the second. He concluded that "passing or failing of 40 percent (of the students) depends, not on what they know or do not know, but on who read the papers," and "the passing or failing of about 10 percent depends . . . on when the papers are read" (p. 3). In another study, Blok (1985) again shows that the same reader reading an essay a second time is likely not to give it the same, or even nearly the same, score.

The unreliability of essay test scores is stressed by other early research (Findlayson, 1951; Pidgeon and Yates, 1957). All tests are less than perfectly reliable, but the studies suggest that the scores on essay tests especially lack the consistency that one would like to see in any assessment procedure. More recent writers have found that the reliability of reading essays has somewhat improved. Reliabilities in the midrange are found in some studies, but these figures are usually lower than reliabilities of objective tests (Frisbie, 1988).

Essay test users do not all write the same types of questions, and some types may be scored more reliably than others. Specific questions over a single concept should provide more reliable scoring than questions requiring a broader, more involved answer (Grant and Caplan, 1957).

To further complicate the problem of reliability of scoring, not to mention validity, the location of the student's paper in the stack has an influence on the score assigned to it by the reader (Bracht and Hopkins, 1968); the first papers read tend to get higher scores than later ones. Several researchers (Daly and Dickson-Markman, 1982; Hughes and Keeling, 1984) have found that a reader's assessment of a paper is influenced by the quality of the previous paper read. The reader tends to judge a paper harshly if it is preceded by a well-written paper; if the previous paper is poorly written, the essay is judged generously. Further, guided reading techniques for scoring do not seem to eliminate this effect (Hughes and Keeling, 1984). Rearranging the papers could very likely give some students a different score than the one assigned by the reader under the current stacking order of the papers. The "previous paper quality problem" is another feature that complicates the reliability (as well as the validity) of scoring essays.

All of this sounds pretty negative, but we first have to see the nature of the problem before we can deal with it. The reliability problems noted here are due to variables that keep readers from applying a set of criteria to the essay's content, making it difficult to produce consistency in scoring from paper to paper.

Scores Influenced by Reader's Expectations

Expectations that the reader (instructor) holds for the student's performance also have an impact on the score assigned to the essay (Chase, 1979). In one study, readers who were led to believe that the paper they were reading was written by a very good student gave it higher scores than readers who were led to believe that the paper had been written by a poor student. Apparently, readers allow their expectations for the writer to color the scoring of the essays.

To further complicate this matter, Harari and McDavid (1973) have shown that student papers with "popular" names on them get higher marks than the same papers when assigned "unpopular" names. Popularity was based on students' choices, teachers' choices, and the frequency of occurrence among two hundred students. Readers are very likely to form expectations for the achievement of students and these expectations influence the scores awarded to a paper.

Expectations the reader holds for the writer also interact with handwriting quality to influence essay test scores. For example, research data on the impact of achievement expectations and handwriting quality on essay scoring show that when writing has low legibility, readers depend more on their expectancy for the student, with the high-expectancy group getting higher scores, and the low-expectancy group getting lower scores (Chase, 1979). When the reading is difficult, instructors fall back on their predispositions about the writer and depend less on the content of the essay.

Other Variables Influence Scores

Physical elements of a paper that distract the reader may lead to a negative appraisal of the content, even though the basic concepts may be correct. The style and legibility of writing, complexity of sentence structure, and neatness are elements that distract the reader and contribute to the ease or difficulty of reading papers. Several early studies show that quality of handwriting, grammar, and spelling (James, 1927; Sheppard, 1929;

Chase, 1968; Marshall and Powers, 1969) all have an impact on the scores given to an essay. Research also shows that writers who use short sentences and words with few syllables tend to get higher scores than those who use long, compound-complex sentences (Chase, 1983).

All of these features support the conclusion that there are variables that impinge on the readers of essay tests as they make their way through the discourse that the student has created, variables that distract the instructor from a common set of criteria being used to assess the essays. To the extent that these variables influence the reader, they have an adverse effect on the validity of scoring.

Limited Content Sampling

The essay test is a relatively small sample of the content of a unit of instruction. Because the test usually is composed of only four or five items, it seems unlikely that it can adequately cover the total range of topics covered in a unit of instruction. A test that assesses only a few selected topics increases the possibility that students may get very high, or very low, scores by the luck of the draw. If student A knows only four topics in the unit and those are the ones on the test, student A will get a good score. But if student B knows everything in the unit except those four topics, B gets a low score. This exaggerated example illustrates the point that when instructors use few items to assess their students, they may well make more errors in ranking than if they use a wider sampling of content. The rather small content sample is a clear limitation of essay tests that seriously affects their validity as a tool for ranking students according to their knowledge of the content area.

Essays Often Promote Poor Writing Skills

Essays are often chosen because faculty believe that students must learn to write, and to do so they must be asked to write. It is certainly true that experience is important in developing writing skills. However, essay tests are probably not an optimal situation in which to teach them. Time limits imposed on the students allow writers little chance to thoughtfully outline the essay or to go back and rewrite passages. Further, our experience shows that few instructors will take time to correct writing errors or to suggest changes in the format or organization.

The testing situation also provides the students with no lexical references, such as a dictionary or thesaurus, to help them express their ideas, and they have no time to research their viewpoint. These procedures and resources are included in teaching students how to write better, but essay test periods are not a good place for students to practice using any of these.

Do Students Do Better on Essay or Objective Tests?

It could be reasonably hypothesized that students study differently for a multiple-choice test than for an essay test. This hypothesis supports the widely held idea that objective tests are confined to facts (where memorization of many details is important), and essay tests focus on higher-level cognitive skills (where integration of materials is fundamental). This idea is not inevitably true, of course. In Chapter Four we provided examples of objective test items that assess the student's knowledge at levels of cognitive demand beyond knowledge. Also, some essay test users include items on their tests that call for a production of facts. Of course, facility with facts and higher-level skills may be found useful in both well-constructed objective and essay tests.

If one sits in the dormitory lounge listening to student groups talking about academic problems, it is very likely that some student will comment on whether he or she does better on essay exams or on objective tests. Many students report that they indeed do better on one type of test than on the other. This hypothesis, however, appears not to be true. Bracht and Hopkins (1968) first asked students to select the type of test on which they did best. When the students later took an examination that included both an essay and an objective part, they did not do significantly better on the type of test on which they said they would excel.

Other studies (Breland and Gaynor, 1979; Hogan and Mishler, 1980) show that the scores students make on an objective test and scores assigned to their essays correlate in the midrange, much like reliability coefficients for essay tests. These moderate correlations indicate a fair amount of overlap between what is tested by essay and objective tests. But data also show an amount of score variation in essays not accounted for by the scores in the objective tests. Some of this variation is no doubt due to errors of measurement, but some must also be due to the different focus of essays. The proper interpretation here is complicated by the relatively lower reliability of the essay test scoring. However, students are ranked about the same by both tests, and their belief that they do better on one or the other seems not to be clearly supported by the data.

Improving the Use of Essay Tests

Now that we have cited some limitations in the use of essay tests, we are ready to talk about dealing with these problems. Because a student should be able to organize information to support a point of view and communicate these ideas within a discipline, we believe that essay tests must be a part of the assessment arsenal. However, we also believe that the essay test is most effective when it is applied according to certain guidelines. Like other types of tests, it must be carefully constructed and used to assess the appropriate instructional outcomes. Here are some suggestions for the most efficient use of the essay test.

1. First and foremost, instructors should restrict the use of the essay test to assessing the outcomes for which it is most applicable. The essay should not be used to test strictly knowledge-level, essentially factual course content that can be better assessed by objective tests. Essay tests should be reserved for assessing outcomes that require higher-level cognitive functions. Here are some suggestions for item formats that are focused in that direction.

- Compare and contrast X and Y in regard to given qualities.
- Present arguments for and against a given issue.

- Illustrate how a principle explains facts.
- Illustrate cause and effect.
- Describe an application of a rule or principle.
- Evaluate the adequacy, relevance, or implication of an arrangement, or materials, and so on.
- Form new inferences from data.
- Organize the parts of a situation, event, or mechanism and show how they interrelate into a whole.
- Sort out the relevant parts as distinct entities from a total situation, event, or mechanism.

A number of questions could be written around each of these formats in any discipline. At the end of this chapter, we provide some illustrations of essay test items in which some of these formats are used. Instructors should think about how the subject matter of their course can be blended with this scheme to invent assessment questions with high cognitive demand. The above list is provided as a guide for doing this.

2. Limiting the breadth of the essay question allows the answer to be relatively brief and specifically tied to a single objective. Broadly stated items, such as "What were the conditions that led to the Civil War?" call on such an array of comparisons between North and South—economics, social structure, religion, foreign affairs, and so on—that the item is difficult to construct in a short time and even more difficult to evaluate. The reader will wrestle with the problems of how many conditions are enough, in how much detail each condition must be developed, and how points should be distributed across the conditions mentioned. It will be most difficult to apply a common set of criteria to each student's production in so broad a question.

A shorter, more specific item can be directly addressed by the writer and easily read by the instructor. For example, the statement "Compare and contrast the role of agriculture in the economies of the North and South at the outbreak of the Civil War" presents a more manageable problem for students and reader than the broader item presented above. This item allows students to focus directly on a single concept and helps the reader to keep the grading criteria more easily in mind, which will improve the reliability of the scoring.

3. All writers should be asked to respond to the same set of test items. Because of time constraints instructors can usually ask only four to six questions in a typical essay examination, which limits the sampling of the many topics covered in the instructional objectives for the unit. Suppose a student knows all the topics in the unit except one, and the instructor asks a question on that topic. The unanswered question will reduce that student's score to 80 percent of total, a loss that hardly seems fair for an otherwise very good student. To avoid this problem, some faculty members allow students to select one item from a set of optional items in place of a prescribed item. This practice is appealing in increasing fairness for students; however, it also means the test is not a common hurdle for all students. If it is not a common task, student scores cannot be compared with each other, and cannot be placed on a common grade scale.

If our measuring procedure involves comparing students on some dimension, as we do with norm-referenced tests, we must ask all students to jump the same hurdles. Otherwise, we have no basis for comparing the performance of a student with others. Here is an illustration. If I am going to sort out the best track and field participant and one athlete runs the 100 yard dash, the 220 yard dash, and does the high jump, while another throws the shot put, runs the mile, and does the high jump, I have very little common performance on which to compare these two performers. Something like that happens when student A writes on questions one, three, and five, while student B writes on questions two, four, and five; instructors have no idea whether questions one through five are comparable in difficulty, centrality of focus on the course objectives, or time demand for the student. This uncertainty gives us little foundation on which to compare scores given to student A and student B in laying out a grade distribution. The soundest way to deal with this problem is to have all students write on the same test items.

The above example applies to the norm-referenced test, which is the most commonly used in colleges and universities. However, the same applies to criterion-referenced tests. If we are going to decide if a student can jump a prescribed number of hurdles, to be fair, each student must jump the same set of hurdles.

4. When students write an essay examination, they should fully understand the overall instructions for attacking the examination as well as the task in each item.

The general instructions should be printed at the top of the examination. They should include things such as what style of writing—outline or complete prose—is required, whether elements such as grammar and spelling will be taken into account in scoring (they should be taken into account only if taught as a course objective), whether organization or quantity of supporting data is the salient feature. The time limit, if any, should be noted.

Beyond these instructions, the wording of the items themselves should point the student toward the answer the instructor expects. How often have instructors heard students say to them, "I didn't know what you wanted there." Some of the jumble of responses instructors get on essays could be eliminated if the writers better understand what the instructor will be looking for in the response. Here is an example:

> *Poor:* Why does an internal combustion engine work?
> *Better:* Explain the functions of fuel, carburetor, distributor, and the operation of the cylinder's components in making an internal combustion engine run.

In the first item, the focus of the task is very broad; students can take a wide variety of approaches to the item but will be uncertain of the instructor's intent. The second item, which presents much less latitude, points the student more directly to the task at hand.

5. Indicate the stature of an item by listing either the approximate amount of time students should take for the item or the number of points it is worth in the total test. This ranking of items gives the students a guide to follow in sorting out the essential elements and otherwise managing their answers, and it allows them to distribute their time across the total test in a reasonable manner.

Following these guidelines will materially improve application of the essay test by helping instructors write better questions and students write better answers. They will also help readers do a better job of evaluating the responses of their students.

Examples of Essay Test Items in Specific Disciplines

The following items, which have been taken from the tests of various instructors, have been judged by the authors as representing pretty good construction of essay items. They are all written to tap skills at the higher levels of Bloom's taxonomy (Chapter Two). They all ask students to organize and analyze information and use it to generalize and to support their conclusions. It is difficult to judge a test item out of the context of the actual course of instruction, but that problem aside, we present these items to the reader as examples of good construction and application.

Science

- Using Newton's third law of motion, explain why a rubber ball bounces higher when dropped from fifteen feet than when it is dropped from five feet.
- Some popular news media have reported that trees themselves contribute to air pollution. Explain this argument and agree or disagree, citing supporting evidence.

Literature

- Contrast the mood of Alfred Tennyson's "Crossing of the Bar" with Dylan Thomas's "Go Not Gently into That Good Night," noting the subject of each and how the poem describes the approach to the subject.
- Compare and contrast the physical traits and the personal character of Grendel in *Beowulf* and Calaban in *The Tempest*.

Social Science

- Two methods for nominating candidates for offices such as U.S. Senator are the party caucus system and the popular

primary. Provide three reasons for supporting each system
and three reasons for not supporting the system.

• Some political candidates call for "getting the government
  off the back of business." What do they mean by this, and
  how is it intended to strengthen the economy of the United
  States?

Reading Essay Examinations

The job of reading the essay is one of the most crucial in the
entire area of classroom assessment. As we have seen, readers
tend to be a bit unreliable in their marking; they are influenced
by halos — positive or negative — given to their students, and they
are distracted by a variety of incidental variables. Our intent
here is to provide some procedures that will help instructors deal
with these problems.

Essay Reading Procedures

Here are some procedures that have proved effective in at least
reducing some of the problematic features of essay reading.

1. Concealing students' names keeps instructors' achievement expectations for their students from affecting their judgment of essays. Before reading the essays, conceal the names
of the students. This can be done by folding over the cover page
of the essay booklet or the corner of the page on which students
put their names.

Or a code system for identifying papers can be used. Students can only put their code number on their papers, and names
and numbers can be listed elsewhere for later matching up of
students and their grades.

2. Before reading the papers for grading, select a few at
random and skim through these to get a feel for what might
be regarded as a "typical" response, for extensiveness of responses,
for topics on which students have done well, and for those on
which they have not. This warm-up is done to orient the instructor to the actual job of reading the exams.

3. Read only *one item* across all papers before going to the
next item. This increases the likelihood that the instructor will

apply the same criteria across all papers. If the reader has only one topic and one set of criteria to keep in mind, it is likely that the application of these will be more even across papers than if the reader has five topics and five criteria to keep in mind while moving across papers.

4. Reshuffle the stack of papers after reading through each item. Reshuffling guarantees that no paper will repeatedly suffer from following a good paper and none will reap the advantage of repeatedly following a poor one. Also, no paper will always be the first or last one read.

5. Use a prescribed reading procedure. There are two in wide use today, the key procedure and the ranking procedure.

In the key procedure, for each question on the test, the reader lays out the ideas that a writer should develop in a complete answer, along with the number of points the student will get for each component of the answer. Then this key is kept at hand as the reader goes through the essays. As the grader encounters a given component in the writer's presentation, the prescribed points for that aspect of the response are awarded. It has been shown (Chase, 1968) that readers using this procedure produce a more reliable set of scores than readers who use no prescribed procedures.

In the ranking procedure, the reader goes through the papers on the first question, laying them in five to seven piles depending on their quality. After the reader has gone through all the papers, he or she may wish to review selected papers in each pile to be sure that the pile does consistently represent the gradation in performance that was intended, and some corrections in placement of papers may be desired. When the papers are finally in place in their different piles, grades will be assigned relative to the order of quality of the piles; the highest marks will go to the top pile, the next highest marks to the next pile, and so on.

Variants of these procedures are also applicable to assessing term papers. Many instructors prefer the key procedure as a guide to reading longer papers. Here the instructor will lay out the topics to be addressed — problem statement, review of research or other background that makes the problem reasonable, plan of attack, and so forth. Finer divisions of expected content are probably desirable, but these illustrate the procedure. As the reader encounters these features, appropriate evaluation of them may be made and points based on an a priori limit can be assigned.

Bluffing

Students will not be able to guess on essays the way they might on multiple-choice tests, but if they do not know an answer, many will try bluffing to enhance their scores. Unchecked bluffing decreases test validity, and, unfortunately, some clever and literate bluffers are hard to catch. Here are some techniques bluffers will use to get some credit even though they do not know the answer to an essay question (Gronlund, 1985). Attention to these points will help the instructor deal with bluffing while scoring a class test.

1. Students will write on every question even though they do not know the answers to all items. This attempt to get an answer on record for each item is sometimes evidenced by the writer's restating the question as a declarative sentence and elaborating on this statement. This is not a response to the question in the test item but rather a way of appearing to have a grasp of the topical content by using the item statement as the evidence.

2. Students may bluff by stressing the importance of the topic in the question, even though they are short of (or missing) facts to support the topic. For example, to a question about the relation between trees and maintenance of air quality, students might say, "This is a vital question in the heavily polluted world of today. Trees have an extremely important role in the maintenance of air quality. They have an essential function in keeping the air breathable." And they may continue on in this vein without addressing the question but, instead, emphasizing the importance of the question. They probably realize this is not a good answer but are hoping for at least some points.

3. Bluffing often takes the form of blatant agreement with the professor on a point, without dealing with the point itself. A broad generalization, without elaboration, might look like this

response by a student who knew the instructor had a special interest in homelessness. "The condition of the homeless is due to the conservative policies of the Reagan administration. This administration has not solved the problem. It still exists and has become a baby at the doorstep of the President." This commentary may have been a statement taken from a recent class lecture, but its veracity is not explained or debated by the student—only reiterated.

4. Bluffers often drop names without details. Suppose a student is asked to take a position on interstate transportation of garbage. The student begins with, "According to the speech by Senator Ecks, this is a complicated problem. This is borne out by Congressman Wye's comments on 'Meet the Press.'" The instructor gets the names, but no details.

5. Writing on related topics rather than dealing with the main point of the question is another technique bluffers use. They load their essays with commentaries that are tied in with the topic, hoping to hit on something that looks worthy and will earn them some credit. "The conflict of Israel and the Palestinians is very much like the situation in Armenia in 1990 . . ."

6. Writing in general terms is another game played by bluffers. Some statements are almost always true and fit a number of situations. "One cannot take everything reporters say in the newspaper as fact. Therefore, one should question . . . " This comment cannot be denied but has no substance in terms of a specific public issue.

Although it is difficult to catch all bluffers in their attempts to embellish their scores, the above items will provide some red flags to watch for while reading essay examinations. Students who are clever and also good writers may be difficult to identify when they are bluffing, and this is one of the problems in the use of the essay examination that has an impact on its validity.

Preparing Students to Take Essay Examinations

Every instructor should spend some time on the communication skills that are expected of students in a course. Although students have met their English requirements, there are usually unique communication skills in a given discipline, many of which will not be covered in a general composition class. This is particularly true of the skills that go into writing a good essay examination. Here are some things instructors can do to prepare students for taking essay examinations.

1. As the instructor moves through the subject matter in a unit, emphasis should be given to the vocabulary that is unique to the academic discipline. The words that convey the ideas, that label the objects, procedures, and so on, are vital to communication in a subject area. They should be emphasized in instruction.

2. Students should be instructed to begin their essays with a true, declarative sentence that lays out the direction of their argument and treatise. A strong opening statement makes the instructor's reading of the essay easier and increases the chances that the reader will look favorably on the rest of the student's response. Readers do *not* look favorably on a student who begins an essay with an apology, such as "I'm not sure of the facts in this matter, but . . . " Teach students to begin their essays with a positive, declarative statement.

3. Students should be encouraged to read all the questions on the test before writing on any of them. This provides the student with an overview of the test and illustrates how the subject matter is spread among the various topics on the test. As the student reads each question, he or she should underline the key verb—compare, summarize, contrast—so that the intent of the question can be addressed without casual oversight. Next the student should make a very brief outline for each question, using single words that will serve as reminders in developing the answer. Once all the outlines are completed, the writing can begin in a more systematic manner. As the student writes on question one, an idea may come to mind that will enhance the response to another question, and it should be noted in the other item's outline. This is another reason students should write those outlines before starting to do any general response writing— so they can be aware of the other items and can add to the response possibilities as they proceed.

4. Instructors should encourage students to write legibly (we have seen the effects of handwriting on grading of essays).

The safest thing students can do is write as legibly as possible; however, because of the time pressure and the anxiety associated with the essay test, students are often not concerned with their handwriting.

5. To promote communication skills, all faculty must emphasize to students that good grammar provides the logic of communication and that poor grammar conveys an inappropriate message. When instructors mark essays in which grammar is a problem, they should write a note to the students, encouraging them to get help with these fundamentals. Most colleges have writing clinics, and students who are serious about their academic (and their professional) careers should promote the skills they need in these endeavors.

6. Instructors can provide a practice exercise in class in which an essay item is given to the students and they are asked to write their responses. Then the instructor and class can discuss the features of a good essay and ways for students to strengthen their responses. In this way, instructors can help students become better essay test takers, a skill for which few students have received specific instruction.

7. Instructors should help students develop the study habits that will enhance their performance on tests. For general essay test reviews, students should be encouraged to study at a moderate level of depth across the entire unit of the test. They should not allow themselves to be distracted by excessive detail but should look for generalizations, connections, principles — and some detail to support them.

While making this review, students should be taking topical notes to use as last-minute reminders of the content. They should note topics on which they feel weakest, those on which they need to understand the principles, and those for which they lack facts to support a position. Then, having completed the overall review, they should go to the noted topics and work on them more intently, integrating the facts into the total topic.

Helping students improve their essay test responses will result in a set of more orderly essays to assess, making the test reader's job easier. And the students may thank instructors for the help that seems not to come routinely from any other source in the system.

Summary

Essay tests are another item in our arsenal of assessment skills. They can be used well for selected instructional objectives but are vulnerable to becoming less reliable and valid than some objective tests. They require care in construction and in reading to avoid the potential limitations.

To avoid problems, the instructor should write specific questions requiring short answers, should not allow optional questions, and should indicate the weight of the items in the total test, by listing the points possible (or time requirement) for each item. The reader should use a prescribed scoring procedure, either the key (in which for each item the principal points are laid out with the score that goes with each point) or the ranking method (in which the reader places papers in piles ranked on their quality).

Students should be given instruction in how to write an essay test. They should begin with a declarative sentence, use details to support generalizations, and always write legibly. Students who do not know the answer to an item will often try to bluff. Careful reading, noting a bluffer's techniques, will help the reader sort out these answers from the honest attempts.

Essay tests used wisely can be an important tool; used casually they can be an infraction of most of what goes into capable assessment.

7

Alternative
Assessment
Procedures

Most faculty continue to use the traditional in-class, closed-book paper-and-pencil exams to measure their students' learning. They rarely have the time or the motivation to investigate alternative assessment procedures. A number of alternative techniques, however, have been used effectively in classroom assessment. In this chapter, we examine some of these nontraditional ways to assess students' learning and discuss their advantages and limitations.

Open-Book Exams

The open-book exam is a variation of the traditional classroom test. Students are permitted to bring and use their textbooks, class notes, and other references. Open-book exams are most often used in classes where the exams consist of mathematical problems that require the use of formulas, tables, or graphs for their solution. But they can be used in other courses where instructors want the students to make use of references in answering the questions. The emphasis in open-book exams is on knowing how to use the references to solve the problems or answer the questions, rather than trying to memorize the formulas or other material. Instructors believe that open-book exams promote a different type of study. Students must be able to apply knowledge rather than just memorize facts. Such exams better reflect real-life situations, where we are able to use references to solve problems.

Students usually like open-book exams. Some research (Boniface, 1985) shows that students tend to be less anxious about this type of test; they also do not prepare quite as thoroughly for them. It seems unlikely, however, that ill-prepared students would do well even if they did have access to the textbook. There simply is not time on most tests for students to stop and look for answers. As one might expect, Boniface's research shows that the students who rely most on using their notes and textbooks during an open-book exam tend to be among the lower achievers and had received lower scores on previous assessments in the class. Overall, Boniface's research shows no clear benefit in levels of students' achievement arising from the use of open-book tests.

As an alternative to the open text and class notes, some professors duplicate and distribute the necessary formulas, equations, and other reference materials as part of the exam. This procedure provides students with relevant reference materials that they do not have to memorize, while restricting access to all the text material. Some instructors allow students to prepare "crib sheets" themselves, with some restrictions, of course. For example, students may be restricted to the formulas they can get on one three-by-five card.

Another possibility is to make only part of the exam open-book. When the authors teach statistics, they prepare exams in two parts. The first part covers knowledge and comprehension of the concepts and principles and is closed-book. When students complete and turn in the first half, they are given the open-book section consisting of problems to solve.

Oral Examinations

Oral examinations that measure students' knowledge of course material are rarely used in undergraduate education today. The greater number of students prevents the use of oral testing the way it was used early in this century. Some selective institutions may still use oral comprehensive examinations over the major as a final degree requirement or for graduating with honors, but oral exams are not often used for regular classroom testing. Their use is restricted mainly to graduate and professional schools.

Oral examinations have many limitations that have resulted in their disappearance as an assessment tool. Because professors must question students on an individual basis, oral exams are a time-intensive procedure. Probably a minimum of thirty minutes per student is required to obtain an indication of a student's knowledge of the course material. Professors do not have this amount of time for testing in the typical undergraduate class. The validity and reliability of oral exams may also be questionable. It is uncertain whether the sample of course material obtained in the allotted time will adequately assess what the students have learned.

If a grade is riding on the results, oral exams put most students under a great deal of stress, causing some students to perform less well than they might on a written test. Students cannot revise their responses, and the instructor has no record of students' performance when calculating course grades, unless the exam is taped, which adds further to some students' anxiety.

The grading of oral exams is subjective. In evaluating a student's responses, professors may be influenced by irrelevant factors, such as the student's pleasantness or attractiveness, verbal fluency, gender, or their own expectations for the student. Students who are facile speakers may be able to respond with glib generalizations that mask real deficiencies in learning.

If oral exams could be used in a small seminar, for example, would they have any advantages? They do provide flexibility lacking in some other types of classroom tests. Faculty can observe students' ability to articulate answers while "on their feet"; they can ask students to clarify answers or to tell more about some topic. If a student seems to know a lot about one question, instructors can proceed to a different one. Bluffing and guessing are also more difficult in an oral exam.

Instructors who want to use oral exams should have a prepared list of questions that they use with all the students. To treat every student equally, they should try to do the same amount of probing for information and clarification with all of them. To improve the objectivity of the grading of oral exams, at least one other person should be present to evaluate the students' answers, which, of course, adds to the cost and complexity of scheduling of these exams. The objectivity of grading would be further improved if the students' responses were taped.

Overall, oral exams have obvious limitations. In the typical undergraduate class, we can recommend them only when a physical disability or injury prevents students from writing.

Take-Home Exams

Take-home exams are popular in many disciplines — philosophy, history, literature, political science — that typically require a great deal of writing. As the name indicates, students are given the exam questions to complete at home. Their written answers are submitted a few days later at a specified time. Students are expected to do extensive background reading, use various reference sources, and produce a well thought-out answer to the question(s). These exams generally consist of extended essay questions requiring the student to integrate and synthesize material and apply knowledge to contexts other than those found in the lecture and readings.

Take-home exams give students an opportunity to explore the larger implications of what they are studying and to answer the questions without the time pressure of a classroom exam. Consequently, the answers are usually better written, longer, and more thoughtful than essay questions written in class. However, test questions may not adequately sample the course material; consequently, students may not master all of the course material, because they are mainly concerned with the part of the content that is directly related to the test questions they must answer. For this reason the take-home exam may not be an adequate substitute for an in-class exam.

The grading of take-home exams presents the same problems encountered with essay tests; it is time-consuming and likely to be subjective. Originality is also a problem with take-home exams. The students may get help from others, so instructors are never sure that the answers are the students' own work.

Surprisingly, many students say they do not like take-home exams. They think they are more difficult and time-consuming and may create just as much anxiety as in-class exams. Students are often unsure just how much time to spend on these exams. They may follow the instructor's suggestions and spend six hours on the exam, but they have no idea whether other students are spending eight, ten, or twenty hours. When instructors use take-home exams, they should set some limits on the amount of time or the number of pages they expect for each answer, and they should enforce these requirements. It would not be fair to tell students to write two pages on a question and then accept a six-page answer from some students.

A popular variation of this type of exam combines the take-home feature with a regular in-class exam. About one week before the scheduled exam, the students are given a list of several essay questions. They are told that the actual exam will consist of one or two questions randomly selected from the list. To improve the content sampling of this method, users should try to develop questions that incorporate as many of the key concepts and the major topics as possible. Students can make use of the text, lecture notes, and other references to prepare adequate answers to the questions. On test day, the instructor presents the questions he or she has selected; to be compared on the same criteria, all students should be required to answer the same questions.

This method has some advantages over the regular take-home exam. Because students do not know which questions will be chosen for the actual test, they must thoroughly study all of the material and be prepared to answer any of the questions. By requiring the students to write the essay answers under ordinary testing conditions, instructors are assured that the work is their own. The in-class essay answers are not as long as those written outside of class, so reading time is not as extensive. To increase the reliability of take-home exams, instructors need to follow the suggestions for writing the questions and for grading that were discussed in the chapter on essay tests.

Repeatable Testing

Should students be able to repeat tests after having received a report of their performance? A number of studies indicate that retaking an alternate form of an exam benefits most students. The use of repeatable tests is not new in college classes. Mastery approaches to learning, such as the Personalized System of Instruction or the Keller Plan, have used retesting successfully for about two decades. Under these plans, students typically have unlimited opportunity to retest until they can demonstrate mastery of the material covered on the unit preceding the test. In this section, we want to discuss retesting in nonmastery learning situations.

Davidson, House, and Boyd (1984) and Cates (1984), who use the retesting option in their psychology and educational psychology classes, respectively, are enthusiastic about its effectiveness. The former researchers make the option available on every test, while Cates permits his students only one retest opportunity per semester. The retests are equivalent, but not identical to the original tests. Both studies report that allowing students to retest helps to reduce student anxiety and increases their opportunity to learn from their mistakes. Davidson, House, and Boyd report positive improvement from the first to the second test approximately half of the time. Cates finds that about two-thirds of his students raise one exam grade through retesting; the mean improvement is about 3.5 percentage points over all the tests.

Some instructors are concerned, however, that permitting students to retest might decrease their motivation to study for the first test. Davidson, House, and Boyd (1984) suggest that this problem can be handled by weighting the two exam scores. In their study, they placed a 25 percent weight on the lower of the two scores and a 75 percent weight on the higher. Cates (1984) allows the students to have the higher of the two test scores for their grade on the one test they could repeat. According to Cates, the retesting option eliminates the need for makeup exams. If students are absent on one test date, there is no concern about the validity of their excuses; in fact, they do not need an excuse. They simply take the test on the scheduled retest date. With the retesting option, there are fewer complaints and arguments about test scores and final grades; students think it is a very fair procedure (Cates, 1984).

What are the disadvantages of repeatable testing? This method requires a large bank of test items from which to develop alternate forms of tests. Thus, a great deal of instructor time and effort are required to write a large number of test items and to collect data to verify that the item forms are comparable in difficulty and in topical sampling. Retesting also increases the number of test papers that have to be graded.

Instructors who plan to use repeatable testing should set a definite time limit for the retest, perhaps three to five days after the original test. This encourages students to keep up in their work and allows the instructor to "close the book" on the previous unit. It is important to require a time lag between testings, however, so that students will have an opportunity to review and to improve their performance.

While instructors should discuss the original test with students, they should not permit them to take copies of any of the tests. Repeatable testing would very soon exhaust the test item bank (and the instructor) if students were allowed to keep tests. Most studies have used this option with objective test items, but it has also been used with essay tests.

Collaborative Testing

An innovative testing strategy provides for collaboration between students on classroom tests. Two collaborative techniques are discussed in the following section.

Group Testing

As the name implies, this method allows students to take tests in small groups of two to five students. Although they consult with one another, the students turn in individual answer sheets. Faculty who have used this method find that it has several advantages. When students disagree over answers, they set about teaching one another the concept in question. And students will not sacrifice their grades; they have to be convinced of an answer they disagree with.

Some instructors worry that less prepared students will be "carried" by the more studious ones. Murray (1990), who reports his experience with group testing, says that this does not happen. He finds that the groups will not let unprepared students use them, and, in some cases, unprepared students are exiled from the groups. When the students who used the group-testing strategy took an individual, in-class comprehensive final exam, they achieved mean scores consistent with their previous group exam grades and with class averages from previous semesters. Murray concludes that the students had learned the material during the semester of collaborative testing.

If multiple-choice tests are used for collaborative learning, test items should be written at the higher levels of Bloom's taxonomy. Knowledge-level questions will not stimulate the kind of discussion that is desired in the groups. The instructor should also check the composition of the groups as far as ability and aggressiveness are concerned. Members may have to be shifted until a mix of students is found that encourages equal participation.

Paired Testing

A technique similar to group testing uses teams of two students each. Hendrickson, Brady, and Algozzine (1987) report an experiment using pairs of students. The instructors developed a series of thirty-question exams divided into two parts. The first set of fifteen questions is taken individually by each student; the second set is taken by teams of two students each. The teams are randomly selected by the instructors and each student turns in an individual answer sheet. The teams are instructed to discuss each test item but are not required to turn in identical answer sheets. The results from the peer-mediated portion of at least two of the tests taken during the semester are significantly higher than results from the individual portion. These instructors believe that by discussing each exam item, students develop a better grasp of the material and also gain more self-confidence.

Journals

Journals, used extensively in English composition classes, are becoming more popular in other disciplines. A cross between a student notebook and a writer's diary (Stanley, 1991), journals alert faculty to students' interactions with the subject matter and their approaches to problems in the discipline. Students are directed to record their reactions to reading assignments and class sessions, to put down the ideas they have trouble understanding, to list questions and speculations about the material, and to look for connections between the course content and material previously learned. Essentially, the purpose of the journal is to increase students' learning by encouraging them to think about the subject matter.

Students usually make three to five entries per week outside of class. Some instructors, however, set aside five minutes of each lecture period for journal writing, when students may be asked, for example, to summarize what they learned in class that day. The instructor may specify approximately the number of words required per entry. Students submit their journals periodically so that the instructor can read and comment on the entries. Frequent checking by the instructor keeps students from putting off the writing and trying to do a week's or a month's work all at once. The format of journals varies; some instructors have students use bound books, while others prefer to have the entries written on loose-leaf paper and kept in a manila folder. The latter permits students to turn in some entries for instructor comments while continuing their journal writing.

Journals may be graded or not graded. Some faculty believe that it is not necessary to grade all student writing (Gribbin, 1991). While faculty may not agree on whether they should grade journals, they do agree on the value of using peer critiquing. Having peers respond to their work broadens the audience for whom the students are writing and provides specific feedback on their thinking. If journals are to be graded, the criteria for grading might include the amount of reaction to the material, the variety of strategies employed, the use of examples and details that show the level of thinking, and so on. Instructors must decide how important the journals are in the course grade; they may only count toward a part of the grade or for all of it.

Leahy (1985) finds journals so valuable that he uses them for the entire course grade in his English literature class. Leahy has students submit their journals in folders at each class meeting; he reads and returns them with comments at the next meeting. The students and instructor jointly develop the criteria for grading and both do the actual grading. He has "journal weeks" during which he places the journals in the department office and every student comes in for at least two hours to read. The students read the folders of the five students that follow them alphabetically on the class roster; the next week, they read the folders of the five who precede them alphabetically. The students also have to read their own journals, write a self-evaluation, and assign themselves a grade. Then the instructor reads all of the peer and the self-evaluations, types out his comments, and confirms or changes the grades the students proposed for themselves. He finds that this is not difficult, because most students are honest and propose reasonable grades. After reading their classmates' entries, most students know how their own writing compares.

Leahy feels that students have much to gain by keeping journals. A student's comment on the journal experience summarizes the potential of this technique: "Looking back through the journal, I realize how much time I've spent thinking about the material covered in this course. And having to write about it, without instructions on what to write, has made me internalize this material. I've had to . . . figure out how this new material fits in with what I already know. This often doesn't happen when the goal of the class is to be able to answer the questions the instructor asks. The journal allows me to answer the questions I *ask*" (Leahy, 1985, p. 112).

Portfolios

A student portfolio has been defined as "a purposeful collection of student work that tells the story of the student's efforts, progress, or achievement in [a] given area" (Arter and Spandel, 1992,

p. 36). The portfolio has been used most often to assess writing in English, but instructors in many disciplines are having students prepare a portfolio of their writing relevant to the objectives of the course. Because portfolios contain a collection of student work, they provide a better picture of a student's achievement in a course. Instead of one big paper in a class, for example, instructors require several samples of writing, including successive drafts of the same work. Thus, instructors can see the processes students go through as they complete writing projects. The kind of writing included in the portfolio varies, of course, with the discipline; faculty try to require the kind that is most representative of the discipline and that will advance the study of the course content. For example, in an English class, the writing might be creative and include poetry, short stories, or literary analysis. A science class might require the development of a research proposal or some kind of problem solving. A speech communications class might have students write speeches that inform or persuade.

To increase the benefits of the portfolio, Gribben (1991) suggests that instructors have students write several short papers focused on specific assertions rather than on general topics, and to write to different audiences and from various points of view. The short papers should be rewritten several times as students expand on their initial drafts, which often are just a search for something worthwhile to say.

Instructors typically collect the portfolios at midsemester and at the end of the term. Written commentary on the contents of the portfolio should be provided, enabling teachers and students to work together to improve students' writing and learning. The portfolios may be graded on a pass-fail basis or letter grades may be assigned. If portfolios are evaluated for a grade, the instructor should use a set of prearranged criteria to apply to the portfolios of all students in the class. One criterion might be the adequate development of an idea through successive drafts, or the like.

Instructors who have used the portfolio method feel it has many strengths for assessing students' writing. Belanoff and Elbow (1986) list the following strengths: a portfolio (1) enables instructors to assess students' abilities to write different types of academic assignments, (2) allows instructors to evaluate students' revising skills, (3) encourages collaboration between students and teachers, and (4) enables teachers to intervene in students' writing processes and ascertain where they may need assistance.

While portfolios typically contain samples of students' writing, they may be used to provide other evidence of student achievement. For example, portfolios may contain art works, such as drawings or paintings; computer programs; dress designs; musical compositions; videotapes of the student dancing or playing a musical instrument; poetry; and so on. The products included in a portfolio are directly related to the learning objectives of a particular course.

Performance Tests

In some courses, students must perform a complex skill or procedure or create a product to demonstrate that they can apply the knowledge and skills they have learned. Designed to measure such objectives, performance tests enable faculty to observe the process of performing the task as well as the finished product.

In courses like art, design, music, home economics, engineering, and the sciences, students are required to produce a product or carry out procedures that reflect the learning that went on in the course. The instructor observes and evaluates the quality of the performance or the product with prespecified criteria.

Preparing Performance Tests

Instructors should begin students' preparation for a performance test with a clear statement of the objective. The objective states what the student should do on the performance test. Clearly stated objectives will help counteract one of the major drawbacks of this type of assessment, namely, subjectivity. Along with the objective, instructors should define the conditions under which the task must be performed. Will the students have access to books or notes? Is there a time limit? The students also need to be aware of the criteria the instructor will use to evaluate their performance.

All evaluations of performance should be guided by an evaluation instrument. Having an instrument ensures that the same criteria are considered for each student's product or performance. Some of the common types of evaluation instruments used with performance tests include the following.

Checklists. Using the objective, the instructor prepares a checklist of all the steps that make up a correct performance, with a space for noting the presence or absence of steps. As instructors observe the student's performance of the task, they simply check off those that occur. If a product is being evaluated, all the attributes the product needs to be acceptable should be listed. Each step or attribute should be phrased in such a way that the evaluator can say either yes or no to whether the student performs each step in the task, or whether the product meets the specifications.

The instructor will need to weight the steps for a grade and set a standard for passing. That is, the instructor must decide if the steps are equally important and how many must be achieved for the performance to be acceptable. The standard is somewhat arbitrary. Perhaps having 80 to 85 percent of the steps checked as accurate is a reasonable standard for passing.

Rating Scales. Whereas checklists restrict observers to yes or no statements, rating scales permit them to indicate the degree to which some behavior occurs or the quality of the performance. Instructors might give an overall rating to a product, or they can rate the various components. For example, speech teachers could give an overall rating to a speech, or they could rate the content, delivery, originality, and so on.

After stating the objective, the professor should list the minimum behaviors that will be accepted as an indication that the student has mastered the objective. A scale of 3 to 5 points can be used for recording the observations. A 5-point scale permits instructors to make finer distinctions about the observed behavior. Exhibit 7.1 shows examples of scales that might be used.

Exhibit 7.1. Evaluation Instruments for Performance Tests.

---

1. *Descriptive — uses words along a continuum.*

Example: Skill in Administering CPR

| Positioning of patient: | Inappropriate | Satisfactory | Optimal |
| Breathing technique: | Inappropriate | Satisfactory | Optimal |

Example: A Still Life

| | Below | | Above | |
| Poor | average | Average | average | Superior |

Color:

Form:

---

2. *Numerical rating — the scale has numerical values assigned to the descriptive points.*

Example: Classroom Speech
  Clarity of purpose

| 1 | 2 | 3 | 4 | 5 | 6 | 7 |
| Poor | | | Average | | | Best |

The more clearly specified the scale categories, the more reliable the ratings. The instructor can grade the student by assigning numerical values to the scale positions, and then totaling or averaging the ratings.

Ratings suffer from a lack of objectivity. The instructor must be willing to take the time and effort to observe students and carefully make the ratings. Using more than one rater and averaging the ratings is preferable, but this is not always possible.

Recent research describes the development of a reliable scoring system for assessing performance in elementary school science (Baxter, Shavelson, Goldman, and Pine, 1992). The researchers developed a scoring guide that lists all the procedural sequences and their rank order according to scientific soundness. The form lists the criteria for each grade and a checklist for the observers, so that all of the procedural sequences can be scored on a common metric (p. 6). For example, to receive an A, a student has to select the right method in the proper sequence, measure carefully, and reach the correct conclusion. If students meet all the requirements for an A grade except care and accuracy in measurement, they receive a B, and so on. Grades depend on the adequacy with which any one of the several procedures is carried out.

Pairs of trained observers independently note the procedures students use and assign a letter grade. The interrater reliability of scores for the observers is above .80, which is quite satisfactory for an assessment instrument of this type. Although this performance assessment is carried out in an elementary school setting, the suggestions for developing the assessment form and carrying out the observations reliably may be useful to college instructors who must do performance assessment.

Advantages and Limitations of Performance Tests

Performance tests provide a way to measure skills and abilities that cannot be measured by paper-and-pencil tests. They are, however, time-intensive methods. Generally, only one student is observed at a time, making performance tests difficult to use in large classes. Having students perform the same simulation and using a student evaluation guide help reduce the subjectivity of scoring these tests.

Evaluating Without Tests

Having students write summaries of textbook chapters and class lecture notes is another way to evaluate students without using traditional exams ("Students Who Take . . . ," 1990). Typed summaries of a page or two are to include the main points in the reading, a critical reaction to the ideas, and a discussion of what is most important and interesting. At the beginning of the semester, the professor sets up groups of four students each, and students stay in their groups for the remainder of the semester.

Each student's summary is put with the summaries of other members of the group in one envelope and submitted to the professor. No summaries can be missed or turned in late. The professor then distributes one group's envelope to another group for grading. The papers are identified only by the last four digits of the student I.D. number, so that students can grade anonymously. The students in each small group alternate on the grading of the weekly summaries, but every student grades at least once.

The graded summaries and a grade report for the professor have to be turned in at the next class meeting. If a grader fails to get the papers back by the next class, 25 points are subtracted from his or her total points for the course. This procedure prevents students from getting behind in reading and grading the summaries.

On the last day of class, students turn in a file containing all summaries for the semester. The professor's grading contributes 35 percent to the course grade, the peer grading accounts for 50 percent, and class attendance the remaining 15 percent. Although some students complain that their peers grade too harshly, the professor says there is a high correlation between peer grades and his grades. Most of the grades earned were A's and B's, but students who skip summaries or do insufficient writing do not pass the course.

Most (90 percent) of the students report that, in spite of the extensive writing, they prefer the summaries over tests. They feel that the learning is more interesting and creative and far less stressful. They also report that they learn more and retain it longer. The professor believes his system encourages more responsibility and produces less stress than do regular tests.

Reading the summaries only at the end of the semester would seem to be a horrendous task for the professor, especially if the class is very large. The professor reports, however, that he uses this method in classes of fifteen to ninety students. He does not read *all* the summaries, however; only a sample of each student's writing is selected for careful reading. There could be a question about the adequacy of the sample and the uniformity of the sample from student to student. Perhaps this is why he gives more weight to the students' evaluations than to his own. There is also some question of how well prepared the students are to grade their peers' summaries. Do they all use the same criteria? Another problem with this method is that the grades are based partly on attendance. Attendance is not usually one of the stated objectives of a course and should not usually be considered when calculating grades.

Summary

A number of alternatives to the traditional paper-and-pencil tests are available to faculty for their classes. Open-book examinations are frequently used. Because these tests permit students to use textbooks and notes to solve problems, they encourage students to learn to apply knowledge rather than memorize material for the test. These tests are somewhat less anxiety-provoking for students than are regular classroom tests.

Oral examinations are not used very often to measure achievement in undergraduate classes because they require too much time. Oral exams allow the instructor to probe a given topic, but they do not measure each student with the same yardstick. They favor students who are glib and handicap students who are shy.

Take-home examinations are used by some faculty who wish to give students discussion questions that will take longer than a class period to manage. Take-home exams present problems that require students to do research and to integrate a variety of materials. However, they limit students to studying only the material directly related to the questions they have to answer, and instructors do not always know if the students received help in answering the questions. In a variation of the take-home exam, the instructor gives the students a list of questions to study at home and then selects questions from the list for the classroom exam.

With the performance test, the instructor observes and evaluates a procedure, a work in progress, or a product that the student develops. For some courses, performance tests are much more appropriate than a paper-and-pencil test. But they are time-consuming to administer and may be difficult to grade. To improve the reliability of performance test scoring, instructors should use at least two observers and a scoring guide listing what is to be observed and the criteria for each grade.

Portfolios of students' written work are being used in many classes. The portfolio encourages active student involvement in and responsibility for the projects to be included in the portfolio. Instructors collect the portfolios once or twice during the semester to check their students' work and provide feedback. This assessment method enables instructors to assess students' ability to write different types of assignments and encourages collaboration between students and instructors. Portfolios are not necessarily restricted to writing but may contain other types of student work, such as art, computer programs, musical compositions, and so on.

Another frequently used assessment tool in college classes, journals encourage students to think about the subject matter they are studying. Several times a week, students record their reactions to lectures and outside readings, list questions and speculations, and try to link the material being learned to other courses or previously learned material. Faculty do not agree on whether journals should be graded or not. If they are graded, the same criteria should be applied consistently to all student journals.

Other alternatives discussed in this chapter are variations on paper-and-pencil tests. Some faculty have students take multiple-choice tests either in pairs or in small groups. Although the students may consult with one another, they turn in an individual answer sheet. This approach encourages students to discuss the material and to "teach" one another, resulting in a better grasp of the material. Another strategy allows students to repeat classroom tests. Those who have used this repeat option report that it reduces student anxiety and increases the opportunity for students to learn from their mistakes. The method does, however, require a large item bank from which to prepare equivalent forms of the tests.

We recommend these alternative methods to college faculty who want new assessment procedures to use in special situations. We caution, however, that many of these alternatives are not suitable for large classes and that they do have limitations in terms of validity and reliability.

8

Administration
of the Test

The careful administration of a test can increase the validity and reliability of students' scores. All the effort that has gone into writing good test items will be wasted if faculty do not provide neat copy, give clear instructions, allow enough time, and prevent cheating. Students should be able to demonstrate under the best possible conditions what they have learned. The suggestions in this chapter will help instructors administer tests efficiently.

Announcing the Test

Students should be aware of *when* tests are to be given. Most instructors put test dates on the syllabus provided at the beginning of the course. If syllabi have not been provided, instructors should announce the test at least one week in advance. Besides knowing the date of the test and the content that will be covered, students should also know the test format; that is, they should be told whether the test questions will be multiple-choice, true-false, completion, essay, or a combination of these. Do students adjust their study behavior to suit the type of test they expect to receive? Research evidence suggests that they do. Lundeberg and Fox (1991) investigated this *test expectancy effect* and conclude that students achieve most when preparing for the type of test they receive. Having information about test format not only helps students know how to study but may also reduce anxiety about the test.

Giving students information about format is especially important on the first test in a class. The first test from an instructor is often the most difficult for students because, unless they have had the instructor in another course, they do not know what to expect. Format information is also important when instructors write higher-level questions. Students are so accustomed to getting knowledge-level questions asking simply for recall of factual information that, unless instructors prepare them, they will complain about the "ambiguity" of the higher-level questions. Instructors must be sure the test reflects what they have told students about its format and content. Jedrey says, "You must be sure that your students get the exam they are prepared for, or are prepared for the exam they will get" (Jedrey, 1982, p. 106).

Test Anxiety

Most students feel some anxiety about a classroom test. A moderate degree of anxiety is motivating and probably enhances test performance. Some students experience so much anxiety, however, that it may interfere with their studying and their test performance. Research consistently shows a substantial negative correlation between measures of test anxiety obtained before tests are administered and performance on those tests. Why do some students experience high levels of anxiety on tests? While failure on earlier tasks influences the development of anxiety, research shows that anxiety does not arise simply from lack of the knowledge or skills required to answer the test questions. Studies show that students with high levels of anxiety do much better on the same cognitive tasks administered under less stressful conditions; they tend to perform at levels similar to students with low anxiety (Hill, 1984). Research shows that the debilitating effects of high levels of anxiety are greater when the student perceives that it is very important to perform well, when the test is expected to be difficult, and when the student may feel time pressure on the test (Crooks, 1988).

There is no magic formula that instructors can use to reduce the anxiety associated with exams, but there are some things that may help. As mentioned above, letting students know what to expect on the test and giving them ample time to prepare are very important to reducing their anxiety. Instructors' perspective on examinations can also play a part in curbing excessive anxiety. Students should understand that instructors are not using tests to "get" students but, rather, to help them learn. Faculty should also avoid overemphasizing grades. If faculty are constantly talking about the importance of the material for the upcoming test, the importance of the test in the final grade, and the importance of a good grade in the course to other courses, and so on, they are going to contribute to anxiety in their students.

Specific techniques that faculty can use to lower anxiety include review sessions, practice tests, or placing exam files on reserve in the library for students to examine. The practice test can be an exam from a previous year but similar in the content, level of questions, length, and so on. The old exams provide students with concrete examples of the kinds of questions the instructor writes, and they can use them as study guides. Strauss and Clarke (1989) find the use of practice tests to be an effective way to help anxious students. About a week before the regular exam and before a review session, they give a practice test as a "take home" and encourage their students to take the practice exam under *test conditions,* that is, working within a specified time limit, without text, notes, or interruptions. During the review session held several days later, Strauss and Clarke display transparencies of the practice exam on an overhead projector and work through the questions, focusing on the process of problem solving and the points critical to getting the correct answer. Students can then ask questions about both the content and the reasoning processes. Because the practice test lets students identify their problem areas and have the experience of actually taking the instructors' test ahead of time, students' anxiety on the real exam is significantly reduced. Clark states that practice tests force instructors to write new items or at least to revise the old ones. They probably also motivate instructors to update lectures so that new items can be written.

Instructors who give essay tests may need to give special attention to preparing students for this type of test. It is worthwhile to take some class time before the first test to tell students how to study for essay tests and how to approach essay test questions. Remember that many students, especially freshmen, have never taken an essay test. In an otherwise humorous article entitled "The Effects of Exam Anxiety on Grandma's Health," Chiodo (1986) lists some of the basic rules he has found successful for reducing students' test anxiety (and improving the health of their grandmothers):

1. Review the scope of the exam.
2. Use practice tests.
3. Be clear about time limits.
4. Announce what materials will be needed and what aids will be permitted.
5. Review the grading procedure.
6. Review the policies on makeup tests and retakes.
7. Provide study help.
8. Make provision for last-minute questions.
9. Allow for breaks during long exams.
10. Coach students on test-taking techniques.

There are a number of books containing information on how to take different types of tests and how to develop the basic skills needed to enhance test performance (a list of these books is given at the end of the chapter).

On test day, a calm and reassuring manner on the instructor's part can help alleviate students' stress. Instructors should encourage students to do well. Remind them to look over the whole test first, so they can plan their time most efficiently. Be sure they understand the directions before they begin and advise them to answer the questions they are certain about first.

In spite of everything instructors do, some students will say they are so anxious in the testing situation that they cannot even think. On occasion, special arrangements may have to be made for these students, such as permitting them to take exams in the professor's office.

Review Sessions

Should instructors schedule a review session for students before their exams? The answer is yes, because a review session is an excellent pedagogical technique as well as an effective way to reduce student anxiety. According to Sahadeo and Davis (1988), a good review session should do more than just repeat information from lectures, answer student questions, or provide hints about what is to be on the test. A review session is a great opportunity for instructors to synthesize the course material and point out the organization and relationships among the concepts so that students can grasp the "whole picture." Instructors instead of graduate assistants should conduct the review, because instructors are better prepared to integrate the material, and their presence is reassuring to students. This procedure also eliminates students' complaints about test questions such as, "The assistant said that wasn't important, so we didn't study it," or "The assistant didn't explain it that way."

The best time for the review is probably the evening before the exam rather than during a regularly scheduled class period. Having the review outside of class saves valuable instructional time, and because the students will already have studied the material, the review will be more meaningful. An in-class review session is boring and frustrating for those students who are not interested; many students will not even come to class on the day of a scheduled review. Review sessions should be optional; the students who do not feel they need the review should not have to attend. Plan to spend about one and one-half hours on the review; this amount of time will be enough to present the overview and to respond to specific student questions or problems.

Assembling the Test

A few test items should be written after each lecture or class meeting. If there is not time to write complete items, instructors should at least write down ideas for questions that can be composed at a later time. This procedure spreads out the labor and also ensures that the important objectives are covered. Instructors are more likely to remember the points they want to stress, and will probably write better-quality items, if assembling the test is not a last-minute undertaking. Sometime before the test, they will want to review the written items for defects that may have been overlooked earlier. It is wise to have some extra items available to replace those that are found to have faults. Of course, the final selection of the items should be made with reference to the table of specifications (see Chapter Two).

Most instructors who use objective tests build up a file of items that can be accessed for later use. If computer scoring and analysis is available, instructors can keep a record of the difficulty and discriminatory power of each item and the effectiveness of the distractors. Using this information, they can leave an item as it is, or they can revise it. When using a test file, the traditional procedure is to write each item on a separate index card. The cards are then selected from the file and arranged in the desired order, and the secretary types the test directly from the cards. This procedure can still be followed, but most faculty will want to make use of their personal computers. Computer programs are available that permit faculty to build a bank of items and to obtain a random sample or a selected sample of the items on command.

If a computerized item bank is used, the test does not have to be typed. As the advertisements for item banking programs say, "Don't type another exam. Ever!" Once instructors have their items in the computer bank, they need only choose the items that they want on the test. Following the selection of individual items, the set of items will appear for a final review. The program then produces a hard copy of the test that should be proofread and then duplicated to produce a copy for each student.

It is a good idea to have a colleague or a graduate assistant read through the test to check for ambiguous questions, inadvertent clues, incorrect keying, unclear directions, and so on. McKee and Manning-Curtis (1982) find that colleague reading is one of the techniques least used by instructors to improve their tests.

The Order of Items

When instructors use more than one type of test item, they should group them by item type; that is, all the multiple-choice items should be together, then all the true-false items, and so on. Grouping improves the appearance of the test, and, more importantly, it helps the student to maintain the particular mental set required to answer particular types of items. Some instructors may want to arrange the items within each item type in an approximate order of difficulty, easy items first and hard items last; others like to arrange items in the order of content.

We recommend beginning a test with an easy item or perhaps one with some humor to it, if possible. Encountering easier items at the beginning of a test puts the students at ease and creates positive affect. It is very discouraging to students not to know the answer to the very first question or questions on a test. Furthermore, when students encounter difficult items early in the test, they may expend so much energy on them that they run out of time before reaching items that they could have answered more easily.

For this reason, when both objective and essay items are used in the same test, we recommend that the objective items be presented first. Students should also be told not to spend too much time on difficult items, but to come back to them later.

Directions for the Test

Clear directions for the test should be *written* at the top of the test. Oral directions take too much time, and students are often too tense to listen. Also, students may want to refer back to the instructions during the test. In addition to the general instructions, specific instructions that apply to particular sections should be supplied at the beginning of those sections. The following information should be included in the directions.

Basis for Answering. The directions for objective tests should first of all indicate the basis for answering. On a multiple-choice test, inform the students whether they are to select the "best" answer or the "correct" answer. We recommend using *best*-answer directions. Although the best and the correct answer should be the same in most cases, there will be occasions under correct-answer directions when students can argue that another option is also correct. If instructors have specified "best" answer, then they can say that while the other option might under special circumstances be correct, it is not the best in that particular situation.

Where to Record Answers. If the test is objective, students must know where they are to record their answers. Answers may be placed directly on the test copy or on separate answer sheets. Most campuses today have facilities for machine scoring of objective tests, and instructors should take advantage of this service if it is available. If machine scoring is used, provide the students with separate scannable answer sheets and instruct them to bring number-2 lead pencils for marking their answers. The scannable sheets with five options per item can be used for true-false and multiple-choice questions, and those with ten options can be used for matching exercises.

Some professors, however, do not use machine scoring for objective tests even when it is available. A student in an introductory course recently showed us the answer sheet she had used for a 100-item multiple-choice final examination. It consisted of 100 short, numbered lines arranged down the left side of a page. The student was to record the letter of the correct option for each question in the appropriate space. We could hardly believe that the professor chose to grade the tests by hand when machine scoring was available. Such a procedure not only required a great deal of time but also introduced a large amount of human error into the scoring, which could have been eliminated by machine scoring.

Essay test answers may be written in blue books that instructors provide the students. If blue books are not used, all students should be provided paper so that the format is uniform.

Students should also know whether any calculations or scribbling should be done directly on the test form or on scratch paper.

Time Allowed. Specify the time limit for the test or for each section so that students can distribute their time most effectively. They should be allowed ample time to do their best.

Unless it is very short (a weekly quiz, for example), a full period should be allowed for the test. Students are not able to concentrate on other materials either before or after an important test, so the time might as well be used for the test. Additionally, longer tests are typically more reliable.

Instructions About Guessing. Students always want to know whether they should guess if they aren't sure of an answer to a multiple-choice or true-false question and whether there will be a penalty for guessing. It will save time if such instructions are put in the directions.

We think it best that students be instructed to answer every item, even if they are not sure about the answer. This does not mean that we encourage random guessing but rather that we expect the students to use partial knowledge to make educated, reasoned, or informed guesses when they are not entirely certain of an answer. This kind of "guessing" requires them to engage in an internal dialogue, develop arguments, and examine consequences (Aubrecht, 1991). Instructing students to answer every item is also the only way to control for personality differences between students that lead some to guess and some to refrain from guessing.

The following is an example of directions that might be used for a multiple-choice test:

> Choose the *best* answer to each of the following multiple-choice items and indicate your answer on the separate answer sheet. Answer every item; there is no penalty for guessing. Do not use scratch paper. You may do your calculations on the test booklet itself. You will have exactly 45 minutes to complete the test.

For an essay test, the directions might read as follows:

> Read each item carefully and think about the re-
> sponse it asks for before you begin writing. Write
> on all questions; there are no optional items. You
> have 50 minutes for the test, so be sure to appor-
> tion your time so that you can respond to each item.

Instructors might even conclude the directions with "Good
luck." This simple message is encouraging and lets students know
that instructors care and want them to do well.

Changing Answers on Objective-Type Tests

Students sometimes ask whether they should change their initial responses on an objective test. The conventional wisdom
is that test takers should go with their first answers and not make
changes. But recent research on this question (McMorris, De-
Mers, and Schwarz, 1987) shows that students can gain from
changing answers. Students who change their answers because
they are able to "rethink the item and conceptualize a better answer" improve their test scores. These researchers conclude that
students should *not* be dissuaded from changing answers.

Duplicating

Instructors should give some attention to the appearance of the
test. An orderly format gives the test a businesslike appearance.
If the test is typed, it should be done neatly, with enough space
between items to keep them from being crowded on the page.
If the test is multiple-choice, keep the stem and all options
together on one page. Essay test questions should also be neatly
typed on a sheet of paper and a copy given to each student.
Instructors should make plenty of copies of the test. In
fact, preparing a few extra is a good idea, in case some test
packets have missing pages.

Administering the Test

The goal of good test administration is to provide and maintain conditions that will enable all students to demonstrate their

maximum level of achievement. Students should never have to feel that their grade was affected adversely by the way the test was administered. The test should be administered by the professor in the regular classroom. Research indicates that the retrieval of information from memory is increased by the presence of the same cues available at the time of learning. Metzger (1979) finds that students' performance is negatively affected when they are tested in a new setting. He concludes that the most accurate assessment of classroom learning takes place in the original classroom. While Metzger is mainly concerned with the physical context of the classroom as a cue, instructors themselves may also serve as a cue to facilitate students' recall of material. An instructor may notice that students often spend test time staring at his or her face; they are evidently trying to remember what the instructor said about something, and the instructor's presence may be the cue they need. It is reassuring to students to have the instructor present—the author can recall as a student feeling disappointed when the professor did not show up on test day. Failure to personally administer the test may send the message to students that instructors do not think the test is very important. Instructors' presence at the test is important for other reasons as well. They need to be available to answer questions and to ensure fair exam conditions.

Instructors should arrive early on test day and organize the test materials (booklets and answer sheets) for efficient distribution. Students should have the maximum amount of time to work. This is especially important in large classes. Students become very frustrated when they have to sit and wait several minutes for the tests to be distributed. In large classes, instructors might want to pass out the tests as students enter the room. An assistant could supervise seating and observe students to prevent talking. Of course, it is important to make sure that the lighting, temperature, and ventilation in the room are within a comfortable range.

Once the test begins, instructors should maintain quiet working conditions, and try to avoid interrupting the students. However, if a student points out an error in the test copy or ambiguities in the directions or the questions that would affect all the students, then make the announcement aloud for all to hear, or write it on the blackboard. Such incidents can be prevented by careful editing of the test.

Instructors should let students know their policy about answering questions during the test and be consistent in applying it. They should not answer questions for some students, and then refuse to do so for others. When responding to a student's question, they should be careful not to give any hints or clues to the right answer. The instructor should only clarify the task for the student.

If there is not a clock in the classroom, it may be necessary to apprise students of the time so that they can pace themselves. As the test proceeds, instructors can periodically write the time remaining on the blackboard. This can be distracting to students, however, and may induce more anxiety. We recommend that instructors give only a single notice that five or ten minutes of working time remain.

Students are expected to stop working when time is called at the end of the test. Some may be reluctant to stop, but fairness dictates that all students stop at the same time. Students who finish the test early should be allowed to leave the room to avoid distracting students who are still working. Moreover, instructors should use the whole period for the test and not plan to have a lecture or present new material following the test.

Should extra time be allowed for certain students? An extra ten minutes or so (until the next class begins) may be allowed for those students for whom English is a second language. A little extra time may be very helpful for these students, especially when reading material is lengthy or complex.

Cheating

Faculty should try to prevent cheating during the test. Recent studies by the Carnegie Foundation indicate that about 40 to 90 percent of today's students cheat on exams or papers, and the number may be increasing. The high incidence of cheating is disturbing but perhaps not surprising, given the "get ahead at any cost" mentality in our society. A college student recently published a book that tells students why they should cheat and how to cheat without getting caught. In a survey of 5,000 professors across the nation, 43 percent say they think that today's undergraduates are more willing to cheat to ensure good grades (Boyer, 1989).

Cheating can take a variety of forms; students may look at a fellow student's answers, exchange information, use a crib sheet, get a copy of the test ahead of time, or have another student take the test. To best deal with cheating, instructors must try to prevent it. There are some procedures that instructors can adopt to decrease the likelihood of cheating. Even though it may make instructors uncomfortable, they should talk with their students at the beginning of the course about the importance of academic integrity. Instructors need to tell students that cheating does not promote their individual learning and that it is unfair to the larger group of honest students. It should be made clear that academic dishonesty will not be tolerated and that those caught cheating will be punished.

Controlling for Cheating

Controlling for cheating is always problematic. When instructors are too obvious with their procedures, it is as though they are sending a message that they expect students to cheat. Instructors want to take steps to prevent cheating, but don't want to act like prison wardens. Being too suspicious may be insulting to the students who are not going to cheat. This can jeopardize their relationship with a class. But if it appears that instructors are not going to do anything to prevent or stop cheating, then some students may give in to the temptation to cheat, and the problem will escalate. Students caught cheating may try to excuse their behavior by saying that other students were cheating and the instructor did not seem concerned or, at least, did not do anything about it. If students know that instructors will punish cheaters, they may be reluctant to engage in cheating.

The following are some things instructors can do to control cheating in their classrooms.

1. Schedule a number of tests throughout the semester. Most students cheat because of the pressure for good grades,

and the higher the stakes, the greater the temptation to cheat. The more tests instructors give in their courses, the less weight any one test has, and the less pressure on students.

2. Prepare exams that are challenging but fair with respect to course material. If instructors make unrealistic demands, such as requiring students to memorize large numbers of formulas, dates, or other isolated pieces of information, they may be inviting students to cheat. Students see this kind of learning as a waste of time and the demands as unreasonable, and they may use these perceptions to justify their cheating.

3. Schedule review sessions before exams to help students get prepared. Announce whether old exams, review questions, or other study materials are available so that all students will have equal access to these.

4. Take steps to maintain the security of tests before the scheduled administration. Do not leave copies lying around the office; keep them in a locked file cabinet. Instructors must even be careful about what they discard in their waste baskets or in the photocopying room.

5. Write some new items each time a test is given, so that students cannot obtain an exact copy of the test ahead of time.

6. On test day, remove the possibilities for cheating by careful proctoring. Proctoring means more than just being physically present; instructors must observe students as they work. They should not read, grade papers, or become preoccupied with other activities during the test. If the class is large, it is a good idea to have a graduate assistant present to assist with proctoring.

If a student appears to have a roving eye, the instructor can stand near that student's desk for a brief time or try to catch the individual's eye to let him or her know that the instructor is watching. The instructor can also ask the student to move quietly to another seat. Singhal and Johnson (1983) say that standing in the rear of the room is an effective technique, because students who want to cheat must turn around to see where the instructor is, and that catches the instructor's attention.

7. Use alternate seats to put space between students. If the class is too large to have empty chairs between students,

instructors should prepare alternate forms of the test. Having alternate forms in adjacent rows reduces the probability of students gleaning answers from other students' test sheets. One alternate form can be prepared by reversing the order of the items; another can be prepared by dividing the test in the middle and reversing the order of the two halves. Alternate forms of multiple-choice tests can be prepared by scrambling the order of the options. It is probably wise to use different-colored cover sheets on the alternate forms so that students know they have different tests. If objective items are stored in a computer bank, instructors can let the computer produce the alternate forms for them. Alternate forms of essay tests can be produced by changing the order of the questions.

8. If the class is very large and instructors do not know the students, they should have them bring photo I.D. cards and display them on their desks. Instructors can walk around during the test and compare the students' names on their cards and answer sheets. This may prevent students having substitutes take tests for them.

The Consequences of Cheating

What do faculty do when they suspect that cheating has occurred? There is no easy way to deal with cheating, but something must be done. Most colleges and universities have specific policies about academic dishonesty, but research shows that faculty do not always follow them. Jendrek (1989) surveyed faculty anonymously at a public midwestern university and finds that approximately 60 percent of the faculty say they have witnessed cheating. When asked what they do about it, 67 percent say they discuss the incident with the student, and only 20 percent follow the institution's mandated procedure, a meeting with the student and department chair to discuss the appropriate action. Nuss (1984) also finds that most faculty prefer to bypass university policy and handle cheating on a one-to-one basis. Jendrek (1989) is critical of faculty taking the matter into their own hands, because it means that faculty serve as the judge and juror and bypass the impartial hearing. Furthermore, if no faculty members report these incidents, some students will be repeat offenders and may, in effect, be allowed to "cheat" their way through college.

If the instructor has suspicions but no proof that cheating has occurred on a classroom test, he or she may want to talk to the offending student privately without involving the rest of the class. It is not always easy to document some forms of suspected cheating, such as wandering eyes or slips of paper. In this case, a warning may be sufficient to curb the student's questionable behavior.

If instructors are certain that cheating has occurred, then the action they take may depend on the seriousness of the cheating. They might give the student who copied an answer or two on a multiple-choice test a zero on that test or let the student take another test rather than bring formal charges. But if the offense is more serious, such as stealing a copy of the test or having a substitute take the test, then faculty should follow the university's policy for bringing formal charges of academic dishonesty against the student. Faculty will, of course, need to substantiate their claim of cheating and present documented evidence to the administration. The university administration should support faculty efforts at maintaining academic integrity by following up with an investigation and appropriate penalties. Wolke (1991) finds, however, that a faculty member cannot always count on receiving this support.

Scoring the Test

Objective tests such as multiple-choice, true-false, and matching can be scored by machine. Machine scoring requires a scoring key, a scannable answer sheet with the correct response to each item marked. The scoring key must accompany the student answer sheets when they are turned in for machine scoring. If instructors prepare the answer key even before administering the test, they are forced to read each question again, and they may be able to identify any problems at this time.

We recommend scoring objective tests by giving one point for each correct answer and zero points for incorrect answers.

The total score is equal to the number of items answered correctly. Some instructors like to use differential weighting, where the items considered more important will receive more points. If some content is judged to be more important than other content, then the instructor should simply write more items on that content. Unweighted scoring saves time and presents fewer possibilities for errors in calculating scores.

Some instructors may want to weight the options on a multiple-choice test. That is, they want to give the correct answer the most points and the other options fewer points depending on the severity of the error. If a student chooses the option that involves the most glaring error, points may even be deducted. These various ways to weight objective test items are more trouble than they are worth, because writing multiple-choice items with differentially weighted options is even more difficult and time-consuming than writing unweighted options. Simple right and wrong scoring, with each item carrying the same weight as every other item, is the best procedure. Aiken (1966) says that the correlations between weighted and unweighted test scores are high, so the weighting does not seem worth the effort. Furthermore, differential weighting adds nothing to the validity and reliability of the test results. Weighting works best with essay tests, where the items can be weighted according to the length of the discussion or the difficulty of the concept.

Another technique some professors like to use is answer justification, which allows students to write a short justification for an answer they feel needs more explanation. The assumption is that students like such an option for questions they consider "tricky." If students are able to give a good explanation of a wrong answer, they can receive a point for that answer; by contrast, they can lose a point for a poor explanation of a right answer. Deducting points for a wrong explanation of a correct answer reduces the number of students using the justification option and does not reward lucky guesses. Dodd and Leal (1988) use answer justification on their standard multiple-choice tests, but they grade only the explanations for questions that the students miss. This reduces their grading time considerably. While Dodd and Leal find that this technique has little effect on an individual student's grade, they find other benefits, the most important being that it reduces students' test anxiety. The students perceive the exams with the answer justification to be significantly fairer than the typical multiple-choice test. The investigators find that the method encourages dialogue between them and their students and helps them to weed out ambiguous questions and to produce better tests.

Dodd and Leal (1988) believe that the answer justification option provides an incentive for students to truly understand the material. The main disadvantage is the additional time required to score multiple-choice tests. They report that it takes an average of twenty additional minutes per exam. Most faculty, especially those teaching large classes, probably would not have this much time for scoring.

As we explained in Chapter Five, we do not recommend using a correction-for-guessing formula, and students dislike the scoring formulas, too. Furthermore, research shows that the rank order of students changes only slightly, if at all, when the correction formula is used (Diamond and Evans, 1973). If an instructor does choose to use one, however, the formula is

$$S = R - W/k - 1$$

where S = the corrected score, R = the number of correct responses, W = the number of wrong responses, and k = the number of alternatives per question. Thus, in a four-option multiple-choice test, the formula would be $S = R - W/3$; for a true-false test, the formula is $S = R - W$. The scoring of short-answer and essay items was discussed in the chapters dealing with those items.

Returning Papers

Students are usually eager to get test results. The importance of feedback in promoting learning has long been recognized. According to Kulhavy (1977), feedback serves two functions: confirmation and correction, with the latter being of greater benefit. Feedback confirms correct responses, telling the student how well the content is being understood, thus helping students to "know what they know." But more importantly, it allows students to know what errors of knowledge and understanding they made and assists them to correct those errors. Anecdotal evidence from students seems to support Kulhavy's conclusion. When students get tests back, they are mainly interested in identifying the questions they got wrong.

The timing of feedback is important. The instructor should correct tests immediately and return them to the students while the material is still fresh in their minds and they can learn from the experience. The tests should be returned by the next class meeting after the test, if at all possible. When there are long delays in scoring and returning a test, students tend to lose interest, which decreases the test's effectiveness as a learning experience.

What form should the feedback take? Research shows that the effectiveness of the feedback depends on the nature of the questions and the correctness of the answers. As mentioned above, simple confirmation of correctness is sufficient for right answers. For incorrect answers to factual questions, the best feedback is simply the correct answer. If the incorrect questions involve the higher cognitive levels, more detailed feedback is recommended. Students need to know the reason for their misunderstanding, and some additional conceptual explanations and discussions may be necessary.

Some instructors merely post the scores and do not return the answer sheets or give any class time to a discussion of the test. Other instructors pass out the answer sheets but do not allow any class time for student questions or discussion.

Friedman (1987) describes his technique for providing immediate feedback on multiple-choice tests. He recommends giving an exam designed to take only about thirty minutes of the class period. The students are instructed to mark their answers on both the test booklet and the answer sheet. At the end of the test, only the answer sheets are collected. The instructor then goes over the exam, giving correct answers orally and answering students' questions. The students know immediately how they did on the test. This method gives students immediate feedback and provides them with copies of the exam, with correct answers marked, that they can use for review on the comprehensive final exam. However, the method forces instructors to prepare a new test each time they teach the course. Also, because the test takes only thirty minutes, it is probably less reliable than a longer test.

A colleague has a system that also supplies immediate feedback without allowing the students to keep copies of the test. This professor places a copy (or copies) of the test on his desk with the correct answers marked. When students turn in their tests and answer sheets, they can immediately look at his copy with the correct answers marked. He says, "I feel that more learning takes place in those few minutes of reading the test items and seeing the correct answers than in any other comparable period of class time." This procedure probably works best with small or medium-size classes. It would be too confusing if there were several hundred students trying to see an answer key.

Another way to provide feedback without returning objective tests is to prepare a transparency of the test. At the class meeting after the test, only the students' answer sheets are distributed, and the test itself, with correct answers marked, is shown on an overhead projector. This procedure not only permits students to see the correct answers to the questions they missed and allows discussion of the test questions but it also helps to protect the security of the test. A less effective alternative for the instructor who does not want to return the test forms is to read through the questions and indicate the correct answers. This procedure takes more time and does not give the students an opportunity to see the other options that were included.

Some professors permit students to keep copies of the test, because they write new items each time they teach the course. In this case, copies of the key can be distributed after the test or posted outside the professor's office. Students can compare their responses with the answer key.

Some computerized grading and record-keeping programs permit on-line feedback. Professors put the test key on the mainframe computer; using their unique passwords, students can call up both a record of their test responses and the answer key. This is a very efficient way to provide feedback, especially in large classes. But letting students keep copies of objective tests means that new test items have to be written each semester. This takes a great deal of time, effort, and ingenuity.

Whatever the method, provide as much feedback as possible so that classroom tests can serve the purpose of promoting students' learning.

Discussing the Test

Although we recommend it, discussing the test results in class can be a stressful undertaking for instructors, who may be letting themselves in for attack from frustrated students. There will be fewer complaints, however, if the test items covered significant material and were well written. Instructors should always be well prepared to explain the keyed answers to students and, of course, should be willing to give points for any obvious mistakes in scoring. But try to avoid either of two extreme postures: (1) remaining intransigent in the face of any and all student objections and (2) easily capitulating to student objections and giving away points as if the testing process were not really important. Do try to avoid being drawn into prolonged and sometimes bitter arguments with students that take valuable class time and bore those students who do not have the same objection.

A variety of strategies can be used in dealing with students' objections to the scoring of certain questions. Instructors can respond with a nondefensive description of why the question is legitimate and why a certain answer is correct. The instructor might ask students who got the question right to explain their reasoning for that answer. If student objections persist, then instructors should agree to consider their argument but defer the decision. It is best that instructors not cave in to student pressure in the class setting. They should tell students that they need to think about the students' objections and to check the lecture notes or text again. Make the decision later, announce it at the next class, and have no further discussion of the matter in class. Another good way to deal with the tough cases is to ask the student to come to the office. The questions can be discussed when the student is not so upset, and no class time will be used.

Another strategy is to have students write out a good argument for the correctness of their answers. Professors can read the arguments and give credit on an individual basis, according to the quality of the reasoning. Requiring written explanations of students' answers avoids giving away points to the lucky guessers who would gain the additional points because of another student's in-class argument. There will probably be fewer student complaints when this method is followed.

Be supportive and not evaluative or judgmental. Never make students feel dumb for answers they have given, and do not ridicule or be sarcastic. Just explain what the appropriate answer is and why. If faculty are supportive, students feel more free to share their reasoning processes in the class.

When discussing essay tests, instructors should try to describe what they expected in a good answer and some of the most common problems they found. They might also select a good answer and read it to the class, but without identifying the student. The best way to avoid controversy over test questions is to write good tests in the first place.

Holmgren (1992) finds that a class-elected group of students, called the Student Exam Review Committee (SERC), is a very effective way of handling students' comments and frustrations, especially in large classes. All students complete a comment sheet about the test and turn it in before leaving the exam. Soon after, the SERC, with access to the exam, the key, the students' comment sheets and their lecture notes and textbooks, meet to go over the exam. They are instructed to identify specific questions that may have been troublesome to the class, and to suggest a form of resolution to these problems. The professor tells them he is interested only in documentation, not idle criticism. After the committee has time to work, the instructor joins them in the room to respond to questions such as "Isn't 'C' (as well as 'A') an acceptable answer to question 21?" "Are you sure that question 18 was covered in the text or lecture?" "We had more than 50 comments on question number 7, can we throw it out?" and so on. Then he explains to the committee what adjustments he will make, if any. The committee members then sign a document stating that, with the agreed-on adjustments, the exam was fair. This document is posted in a place for all students to see when the exams are returned to the class. The students in his class respond very favorably to this opportunity to make comments about exams through class representatives who act on their behalf. The professor likes the exam committee plan because it provides a way to respond to students' frustrations without disrupting the entire class, and he is able to get a fair and unemotional evaluation of the exams. He writes, "I won't return another exam to a large lecture section without the invaluable insight I receive from these students" (Holmgren, 1992, p. 216).

Missed Examinations

Faculty should inform students early in the course about their policy on makeup exams. Some faculty do not permit missed exams to be made up for any reason. They calculate the final grade for those students on the basis of the scores they have, using differential weighting so that the maximum possible score is the same for all students.

Other instructors permit makeup exams if the student has been ill or has a legitimate reason for missing the test. How should instructors handle makeup exams? If the student can make up the exam immediately, before it is returned and discussed with the class, and before fellow students can be coerced into divulging answers, then instructors might even use the same test. It is probably best, however, to prepare another form of the test. This form, of course, should cover the same material and be equally difficult. Preparing another test is not an easy task, especially for a rather lengthy multiple-choice test, unless instructors have an item bank from which they can select an item sample comparable to the one on the original test. In preparing an alternate form, it is important to go back to the table of specifications to make the alternate test comparable to the original.

Student Evaluations of Exams

It is a good idea to obtain feedback on exams by having the students evaluate them. Instructors can ask if the questions were stated clearly and if the content and format were what students

Exhibit 8.1. Student Evaluation of Test — I.

Use the separate answer sheet provided to indicate your responses to the following items. Please return at the next class meeting.

1. Overall, I would rate this test as
   a. Excellent   c. Fair
   b. Good   d. Poor

2. How well did the test correspond to your expectations?
   a. It was exactly what I expected.
   b. Some of it was what I expected.
   c. It was not at all what I expected.

3. The test questions
   a. Represented the content of the text quite well
   b. Were not representative of the content of the text

4. The test questions
   a. Represented the content of the lectures and discussions quite well
   b. Were not representative of the content of the lectures and discussions

5. The test was
   a. Too long   b. About right in length   c. Too short

6. The test was
   a. Too hard   b. About right in difficulty   c. Too easy

7. Most of the test questions were
   a. Challenging   b. Somewhat challenging   c. Not very challenging

8. Most of the test questions were stated clearly.
   a. Agree   b. Undecided   c. Disagree

9. There were too many trivial questions on the test.
   a. Agree   b. Undecided   c. Disagree

10. How well do you think you did on this test?
    a. Very well (at least 90% correct)
    b. Average
    c. Not very well (fewer than 70% correct)

11. How would you grade this test in terms of its form, content, and fairness?
    a. A   b. B   c. C   d. D   e. F

12. How do you think this test could have been improved?

13. What changes would you like to see made in the next test?

Exhibit 8.2. Student Evaluation of Test—II.

Use the separate answer sheet to indicate your responses to the following items. Return at the next class meeting. Indicate the extent to which you agree or disagree with the following statements. Use the following key:

        a. Strongly agree   d. Disagree
        b. Agree   e. Strongly disagree
        c. Undecided

1. Most of the test questions were clearly stated.
2. The content I expected to see appeared on the test.
3. I was satisfied with my answers to most of the test questions.
4. Overall, I thought this was an excellent test.
5. This was not a fair test.
6. The test covered the most important aspects of the course.
7. There were too many questions covering trivia.
8. The test accurately assessed what I studied.
9. The test questions challenged me to think.
10. The test was too long for the time allotted.
11. The test was too difficult.
12. I think I did well on this test.
13. One could do well on this test just by cramming.
14. The test did not accurately assess the content I learned.

Open-Ended Questions:

15. How do you think this test could have been improved?
16. What changes would you like to see made in the next test?
17. How would you grade this exam on an A to F scale?

---

expected. Obtaining student comments provides instructors with useful information and helps the students feel more like partners in the learning process. Two sample evaluation forms with slightly different formats are shown in Exhibits 8.1 and 8.2. These forms are based on one suggested by McMullen-Pastrick and Gleason (1986). With the exception of the open-ended questions at the end, the forms shown here have been designed to be machine scannable. Of course, if the class is small, instructors might want to prepare an evaluation form that has all open-ended questions.

    The instructor can distribute the evaluation forms to students after they finish the test and either have them complete the forms on the spot or take them along to be returned at the next class meeting. The latter is preferred because the students will have time to calm down after the test and be more objective about it.

An evaluation is especially helpful after the first exam in the course, when the class could still benefit from changes or improvements in the tests. The summative evaluation used at the end of the course should also contain some statements about the exams, feedback, and grading procedures.

Summary

Testing involves more than writing items and calculating grades. In this chapter we looked at some of the practical problems involved in the administration of the classroom test. Administration is an important part of the testing process, because the way in which tests are administered can affect students' scores. We do not want test administration to detract from an otherwise good test.

The dates of all tests should be announced well in advance, preferably in the syllabus. Students should be told the content and the cognitive level of the questions and the test's format. Students perform better when they study for the kind of test they will receive, and they experience less anxiety when they know what to expect. Getting students involved through practice tests and review sessions helps them learn and contributes to the reduction of test anxiety.

Write out complete directions on the test copy including the time available, the basis for answering, where to record answers, and instructions about guessing. If the test is true-false, multiple-choice, or matching, machine-scannable answer sheets are very convenient. Scoring on these tests should be kept as simple as possible; one point for each right answer, with no correction for guessing, is the recommended procedure.

Every effort should be made to provide good testing conditions so that students can do their best work. Instructors should be present to administer the test. Their presence is reassuring to the students, and it may deter some students from cheating.

Suggestions were made on how instructors can prevent cheating on their tests and how to deal with the problem, if it should occur. Test results should be returned as soon as possible, and instructors should provide some time for discussion so that students can learn from the testing experience.

Books on Acquiring Test-Taking Skills

Annis, L. F. *Study Techniques.* Dubuque, Iowa: Brown, 1983.

Dobbin, J. E. *How to Take a Test.* Princeton: Educational Testing Service, 1981.

Feder, B. *The Complete Guide to Taking Tests.* Englewood Cliffs, N.J.: Prentice-Hall, 1979.

Geoffrion, S. *Get Smart Fast: A Handbook for Academic Success.* Saratoga, Calif.: R & E Publishers, 1986.

Gilbert, S. *How to Take Tests.* New York: Morrow, 1983.

9

Computer-Assisted Testing

Virtually every scholastic discipline has embraced the computer and found it almost indispensable. The sciences and mathematics came first, and social sciences have quickly followed. Even the fine arts now find the computer a time- and effort-saving tool. The business of assessing the educational outcomes of instruction is in the mix, also. Computers are used not only to create tests but also to administer them and interpret results to test users. Computer systems can provide immediate feedback to the test taker, can select the next item to be presented based on how well the examinee did on the previous item, and can store and analyze results for future use in course planning and test construction. Clearly, the testing operation can exploit the possibilities that computer systems provide.

In this chapter we look at the computer as a test administration aid, the use of computers for banking test items, and test laboratories with hard copy tests — scored and analyzed by computers.

Computers as Delivery Systems

In the earliest application of computers to testing, they were used to deliver test items in much the same manner as did hard copies of tests. The system worked like this. The student sat down at the terminal and put in certain I.D. data. The computer checked this against the class roll and either accepted or rejected the student as a test taker. When the computer approved the student I.D. data, it presented on the screen of the terminal the first item on the test. (Most testing by computer has dealt with the multiple-choice format.) The student selected an answer and depressed the appropriate key on the computer to record it. The computer then presented the next question. This procedure continued until all items in the test were administered.

Although we have said that the computer presented the items in order in essentially the manner of a hard copy paper-and-pencil test, computers have the facility to go beyond the capability of most hard copy. For example, computer graphics can be used to present diagrams or to effect motion: a geometric form can be rotated; a plant part can be seen from more than one angle; the trajectory of a cannon ball can be illustrated in motion. These features are a chore to get programmed into the test delivery, but they are definitely possible.

In some programs, students are given immediate feedback on each item. As the student records the response to the item, the computer prints on the screen whether or not the student's answer is correct. In a few early programs, if the student missed the item, an explanation of the error was provided and the correct response noted, making the test not only a measuring device but also an instructional tool. Some computer test users also experimented with allowing the test taker who missed an item to select alternative options until the correct answer was located. The score then was the number of attempts taken to reach the correct answer. Lower scores got the highest grades, while high scores — reflecting many attempts to reach the correct answer — received the low grades.

Providing students with feedback seems to be a good instructional procedure. However, providing test takers with immediate feedback may contribute to their test anxiety (Wise and others, 1988). This finding is causing computerized-test users to rethink their methodology. Apparently the use of item-by-item feedback should be discontinued until further research discovers how to manage the problem of test anxiety.

The computer presents the test problems and keeps track of the item-by-item responses. Each student is given a total score upon completing the test. Also, item data are stored and will eventually provide item analysis information, class averages and spread of scores, and a class roster for the instructor.

This is the simplest application of computers to test administration. The computer simply does the administration, the record keeping, and the statistical work for the instructor, chores from which most instructors would like to be relieved. However, the computer is capable of doing more complex testing operations.

Adaptive Testing

Computerized testing has recently taken a new direction in exploiting the facility of electronic devices. First test items are pretested and item difficulties are determined. A large pool of items is accumulated on a given topic, and these items are stored in the computer memory. The student sits down at the computer, types in the course number, his or her identification number, and a code to start the test. The computer checks all these data, and if it decides that this is a legitimate student in the class, the testing process begins. The computer randomly selects an item from the pool of items stored in the computer and presents it on the screen. The student reads the item and responds on the keyboard of the computer. If the student's response is the correct answer to the item, a slightly harder item is then selected from the pool and presented. If this item is failed, a slightly easier one is provided for the student. This procedure is continued until the student's highest level of performance, in terms of item difficulty, is established. Here a criterion is set, like five items correct in a row, or five out of seven items, or the like. When the student reaches this criterion, the test is terminated.

Student performance is evaluated on the basis of the level of difficulty reached, not on the traditional number of right answers. For some students, it may take only a small number of items to establish their performance level, while others may take a larger number. Hence, the number of items attempted by one student may be quite different from another. In this situation the number correct does not have the same meaning as if everyone took the same number of items as is done in traditional paper and pencil tests.

The biggest problem in adaptive testing is the development of the item pool. Pools must be large, including maybe a hundred or more items on a given unit of work and possibly hundreds across an entire course. To complicate the matter, items in the pool must be pretested to establish their difficulty levels. Not all samples of students will have the same abilities in the subject for which we are building test items. Because of this, when one item is pretested on a different sample of students than another, conventional indices of difficulty may well not be comparable from item to item. Consequently, items pretested on different samples of students will very likely not be as consistent in their level of difficulty if they are computed by conventional procedures. Even if the ability of students in a class may be very similar from semester to semester, some precision is lost when different groups are used to establish difficulty indices. We must here assume that the abilities of the various samples of students were the same, an assumption that is probably not entirely true.

A procedure based on what is known as item response theory (IRT) is used by some testers to compute the item difficulties. This procedure is attractive because it claims to place item difficulties on a common scale, even though the items are pretested on different samples of students with varying levels of ability. Thus, items can be added to the pool at any time, without losing precision in the difficulty index. The actual procedures of IRT are beyond the scope of this book but may be found in more specialized sources. The Rasch model is one popular foundation for IRT methodology.

Advantages of Adaptive Testing

We have already seen some attractive aspects of adaptive testing, but not all of them. Here are some of the most widely cited advantages.

1. Tests may be given on demand. Since no two tests will be alike, students do not all have to take the test at one time. Test items selected by the computer will vary from student to student, depending on the test taker's facility and the computer's selection from the pool. However, the difficulties will be on a common scale for all tests, so each test will identify a given student's ability at the appropriate level of complexity.

2. Retesting of a student is possible because the second test will likely be made up of different items than the first. Retesting may be considered, especially if the student has been given a chance to improve the necessary skills in the meantime.

3. Tests are taken at the student's own rate of work. Students may finish and leave the terminal on their own schedule.

4. Test security is less of a problem than with paper-and-pencil tests. Because the test item pool is stored in the computer, it is not available to the searching eyes of a casual visitor in the faculty offices. A clever computer student could "break into" the computer's memory, but it may not be worth the trouble. No student knows, or can discern, which items in the pool the program will select, so it is difficult for a student to "steal the test." And if a student learns the answers to all the items in the pool, chances are good that the student has learned the necessary content for a given unit of instruction.

5. Adaptive testing is time-saving. It takes up to 50 percent less time to take a computerized, adaptive test than a traditional paper-and-pencil test. Items that do not contribute to setting the students' upper level in difficulty are not administered in adaptive testing. For this reason students do not waste time taking items they can easily pass or contemplating guessing strategies for items they clearly cannot answer correctly. Interestingly, this reduction in time does not appear to materially affect the reliability of the test.

6. The test can be adapted to a wide range of ability, because it selects items based on the student's performance. Capable students will be administered items with relatively high difficulty levels, while less capable ones will get items of lower difficulty. Also, adaptive testing can be set up to deal with criterion-referenced tests, where items are pitched at a given level of difficulty.

Problems with Adaptive Testing

In spite of its advantages, adaptive testing is not without limitations. Users must weigh the advantages against the limitations before jumping into this test delivery procedure.

1. The preliminary work for developing a system is considerable. The items must be written and pretested. IRT systems require fairly large samples of students from which to determine item difficulties. Items that do not stand up under item analysis will have to be replaced or revised and tried again. The sheer number of items necessary to create an adequate item pool requires that the process be started well in advance so that the necessary trial of all items can be completed before the start-up date. Allowing sufficient lead time is of great importance.

2. Developing an adaptive testing program (or any computer-based program) is expensive. Purchasing dedicated equipment and employing technical personnel is costly at the outset, but the testing share of these costs can be offset by using electronic equipment in several classes or for other computer applications and training between tests. However, sharing computers with other users may cause scheduling conflicts and other frictions over who controls what. Each set of users will have certain priorities, which may not be compatible for all users. Testing programs with their own computers are always the smoothest operating systems, but they also carry the largest price tag.

3. Students who use the computer in adaptive testing must be minimally literate in the use of computer terminals. Most students today have some skill in this area, but the range of skills will vary widely. Instructors must be sure to instruct students on how to initialize the program and how to operate the computer to respond to the test, for example. If students must struggle with the computer, it will distract them from concentrating on the test. For adaptive testing, the necessary computer skills are few and can be acquired with a minimum of coaching. Training should be planned as part of the preliminaries for setting up the program.

4. Since the IRT data in which test results will be reported will not be familiar to test users, meaningful ways to convey the results are difficult to devise. Students like to see scores that

show the number or percentage of correct answers and their ranking in the class. Scores in adaptive testing are tied to levels of difficulty. Devising a grading procedure for these data is a new and potentially puzzling process to faculty and students alike. The usual procedure of breaking the distribution into percentages will not work, but interpreting the scores in terms of "can do–can't do" matters is very useful as a guide for student review and for further instruction.

Alternative Electronic Facilities — The Test Lab

The need for a set of dedicated computer terminals makes computerized testing a problem for many intended users. However, there is a modification of the procedure that has been tried by some institutions with considerable enthusiasm on the part of their faculties. This is the electronic testing laboratory.

Here is how it works. A room with forty to fifty desks (testing stations) is set aside by the institution for the exclusive use of test administration. Instructors reserve blocks of time for their students to take tests in the laboratory. Each student in a class that has come to the end of an instructional unit makes an appointment to go to the lab within a given time frame, usually within two or three days. At the appointed time, the student appears and presents his or her I.D. card, and appropriate identifying data are put into the computer by the room monitor. The computer then checks the enrollment of the student in the class being tested. If the computer report on the enrollee is positive, the student checks all books, bags, and other personal items and proceeds with the test.

The laboratory monitor has been provided with a set of five to six "equivalent" forms of the test by the instructor. These are printed copies like those that might be used in a typical classroom. The computer is asked to select a form of the test at random. The monitor then gives the student the computer-selected form, along with a machine readable answer sheet and a number-2 pencil. A testing station is also assigned to the student, who goes to the appointed station, sits down, and takes the test, very much as it would be done in a typical classroom.

When the student finishes the test, it is turned in to the lab monitor and immediately fed into an optical scanner that reads the test into a computer. The computer prints out a short report for the student, including the student's score on the test, subscores on groupings of items — if the instructor desires — and a summary of the student's previous tests during the term. The item data and student's score are stored for later item analysis and reporting to the instructor on the class performance.

In some cases, instructors allow students to retake an exam at the laboratory after they review course materials. The computer checks to see that a second form of the test is selected for retesting. Students are usually required to take the second score, whether or not it is higher than the first.

To utilize the laboratory, an instructor must be prepared to develop several forms of the examination over each unit of course work, a procedure that requires a large item bank from which items of equivalent difficulty can be drawn. Students who are accustomed to taking tests in their classrooms will need some orientation on the procedure. The testing laboratory also will have to be reserved well in advance of the test at most institutions. Class rosters with appropriate I.D. numbers should be supplied to laboratory personnel, so that students who come to take their tests can be appropriately identified; in addition, students must be advised to take their student I.D. with them so that laboratory personnel can admit the right persons to the test.

The laboratory approach is most beneficial in dealing with very large classes, which present the greatest challenge to testing in regular classroom settings. Large classes are difficult to monitor; the logistics of distributing and collecting tests are complex; getting to a student to elaborate on instructions, and so on, is often next to impossible without disturbing other students. All this makes testing of large classes difficult in a lecture hall. The testing laboratory can be a reasonable alternative that not only manages these problems much better than traditional methods but also permits retesting and immediate feedback to students. Also, no class periods are used for testing (although some instructors dismiss one class during testing). If no class time is taken up in testing, it allows for an additional lecture during the time testing would have been going on in the classroom.

If students do not keep their lab appointments, some institutions require them to pay a fine, and, in some cases, student fines go far toward covering the cost of operating the lab. Imposing fines is not universally endorsed; each institution must work out its own procedures that fit the philosophy of the institution.

However the lab is finally formulated, it provides an economical alternative to computerized testing that still capitalizes on the use of electronic hardware to facilitate testing. It relieves the class instructor from administering and monitoring the test, two difficult chores in large classroom settings. It also controls unwanted collaboration between students in large classes, where little space is available for conveniences like alternate seating. Also, retesting is possible if the instructor wishes to allow it.

Unfortunately, there is no escape from constructing a large item pool. At least four to five times more test items must be prepared than will appear on any one test form. Many instructors who have taught a given course and have written new items each term will have a collection of items on hand. Like the item pool for adaptive testing, lab test items should have a difficulty indicator that can be used to formulate equivalent forms. Again, IRT can be used to develop difficulties on a common scale — or nearly so — for all items in the pool. In any case, some objective base should be used to indicate the difficulties of test items so that test forms may be equated before being presented to the students. A subset of test takers should not be given a special advantage simply because they were given an easier form of the test than other students were.

Summary

In this chapter we presented several adaptations of electronic equipment to the problem of classroom testing. The simplest of these uses the computer as a standard test delivery system to present the test item by item. Each item may be scored and students informed of their progress as they proceed, or the test score is immediately presented at the end of the test.

A variation of this system is known as adaptive testing. Here the student is given an item from the pool of items on the instructional unit. If the item is answered correctly, a harder item is selected from the pool; if the item is missed, an easier item is selected. In this manner, the student's difficulty level for performance is established. Students are ranked on the difficulty level at which they are placed, not on the number of correct items.

The computer laboratory has been devised as an alternative to large-class test administration. Here students appear at an appointed time to take a randomly selected form of the test, chosen from five or six forms provided by the instructor. The student takes the test by filling in a machine-readable sheet that is immediately scored, and a test report is run off for the student by the computer. The test lab obviates the difficulties of testing in large classrooms, provides immediate feedback for the student, and allows a repeat testing for the student if desired. It also does not use class time for testing, permitting the instructor to use the time in another way.

The computerized applications listed in this chapter are the most widely used and discussed in the testing business. The presentation is not intended to be exhaustive but to present the basic paradigm for computerized testing.

10

Item Analysis

After instructors have written a set of test items, following all the rules, they still do not know if the items will show which students have mastered the topics of instruction and which have not. The items must be tried out on the students before the instructor can determine how well each item works. This procedure of judging the quality of test items by examining the students' responses to them is called item analysis.

An item will be marked incorrectly by students who are generally weak in a content area but will be marked correctly by students who are strong in the area. Item analysis is a set of techniques that will help instructors find out whether their test items separate the competent students from the less competent ones. It will also indicate how hard the items were for the students. The first task of item analysis is called *item discrimination,* and the second is called *item difficulty.*

How Item Analysis Is Done

Because item analysis requires data on the test, the procedures described here require that the test first be administered to see how students respond to the various items and what their total scores are. Students' responses to the separate items and to the total test will be the data used in doing the item analysis.

There are several ways to do an item analysis, and we look at two of these. First, we look at item analysis as done by a computer, and second, we see how an item analysis can be done less formally by hand. Both have their advantages, and, depending on the availability of electronic data services, professors may choose one or the other.

Electronic Item Analysis

If someone is measuring the height of a number of people with a ruler, the values must sort the tall people from the shorter ones, or we would have no confidence in the measurements. Similarly, a test item must sort the students who know the topic well from those who do not. That task is called item discrimination.

One way to approach item discrimination is to correlate the performance of students on a single test item with their total test performance. If an item correlates well with the total score on the test, then the students who got the item correct tended to do well on the total test (that is, they know the topic well); and those that missed the item did poorly on the total test. Of course, item scores from a multiple-choice or true-false test will have only a small range (1 if right, 0 if wrong), while total test scores will have a much wider range. Nevertheless, we can correlate these two sets of data and get useful correlation coefficients. (The point biserial correlation coefficient rather than the standard correlation is used because the items are scored dichotomously, but interpretation is the same.)

In a brief discussion in Chapter Three, we noted that a correlation requires two scores for each student. In discrimination analysis, the first score will be a correct or incorrect item (usually 1 and 0), and the second will be the total score on the test. The example below shows data for one item on a thirty-item test (of course, we have too few students, but it suffices for the illustration).

	Students					
	Ann	Bes	Cal	Don	Efy	Fay
Item 1 score	1	1	1	0	1	0
Total score	25	19	18	16	12	10

The two measures we shall use to do an analysis of item 1 are the item score (1 or 0) and the total test score. For example, Ann got item 1 correct and got 25 points on the total test — two scores for Ann; Bes got item 1 correct and got a total score of 19, and so on. We now correlate these two measures across the entire class and come out with a coefficient for item 1 on the test.

In the above set of data, we can see that the students who got the item correct tend also to get the higher total test scores. The average total score across the persons who got item 1 correct is 18.5, while the average total score for the missers is 13. This shows that the item is to some extent related to the total score — the ones who got it correct tend to score above those who missed it. In fact, the correlation between these two data sets is .53 — a rather middling correlation. It says that as students get higher scores on the total test, their probability of getting the item correct goes up, but the relationship is at best moderate. A positive correlation of this magnitude, however, says that the item is definitely contributing to the function of the total test; that is, this item separates the students who knew the topic well (as shown by their total scores) from those students who knew it less well. An example of how a computer analysis might look is given in Exhibit 10.1. The data here represent another test taken by the same set of students.

Exhibit 10.1 shows data on three items from a much longer multiple-choice test with three response options, A, B, and C. The r values represent the correlation of an option with the total score on the test; the p values are the percentage of students who chose that option (the p value shows how difficult an item is; we will discuss item difficulty later). In Exhibit 10.1, the asterisk (*) indicates the option that is correct.

Now look at each item. In item 1, the correct answer, B,

Exhibit 10.1. A Section of a Computer-Produced Item Analysis.

	A	B	C
1.	$r = -.27$	$r = .25^*$	$r = -.06$
	$p = 13.89$	$p = 50.00$	$p = 36.11$
2.	$r = -.46$	$r = .49^*$	$r = -.22$
	$p = 5.56$	$p = 88.86$	$p = 5.56$
3.	$r = -.30$	$r = -.13$	$r = .34^*$
	$p = 16.67$	$p = 27.78$	$p = 55.56$

correlated with the total score at .25, not high, but positive, showing that the high scorers on the total test were just slightly more likely to choose the right answer than were the low scorers. This low correlation means that the quality of item 1 is suspect. Notice that the correlations on the distractors A and C are negative. This means that the students who chose these incorrect options tend to be among the low scorers on the total test. This is how we want the data to come out. Correct options should show positive correlations, while the distractors should show negative correlations.

In item 2, the correct option is also B. The correlation is .49, a fairly good correlation with the total. Again, notice that the distractors (A and C) correlate negatively with the total score, just as we hope they will. Item 2 is a pretty good item.

In item 3, the keyed option, C, correlates with the total test score at .34. This is a modest correlation, but clearly positive. The distractors correlate negatively with the total; although not large, the negative correlations clearly point to the probability that the students who chose these wrong answers were among the low scorers on the total test.

In general, although item 1 is a little weak, these three items are doing the job we ask them to do, that is, sort the students who know the material from those who do not. In this example, no one item does this job superbly, but each is contributing to the total task we assign to this test; that is, all have some power to sort students who know the material from those who don't.

Using Item Analysis Data

When the instructor wrote the test whose first three items are shown in Exhibit 10.1, he or she believed that all of the items were well constructed and would do an adequate job of assessing the outcomes of instruction that were laid out in the table of specifications. The item analysis showed that the first three items seem to be doing well enough; however, not all items in a test will do the job of sorting the "know its" from the "don't know its." What shall we do with these items?

Some faculty believe that items that perform poorly should be eliminated and a second scoring done. Since these items are not operating as the instructor had hoped, this procedure seems reasonable. However, faculty must keep in mind the matter of content validity. The test is supposed to cover the topics of the course with the emphasis that is indicated in the course objectives. If the instructor eliminates too many items on a single topic, the test no longer samples that area and, consequently, loses some of its content validity. However, if the items in that area are doing a terrible job (with correct answers correlating with the total at, say, .15, .10, or lower—and in some cases even negatively), then the course content area is not being assessed very well anyway. It therefore seems reasonable to drop those unacceptable items from the scoring—but be sure the items are really bad before doing this.

The standard error of a correlation coefficient can help an instructor decide objectively whether or not the data show an item to be really unacceptable. It is calculated by the formula:

$$\text{Standard error} = \frac{1}{\sqrt{(\text{number of students} - 1)}}$$

As used here, the standard error is a kind of yardstick that instructors can use to decide how much larger than zero a correlation coefficient should be before selection of the right answer is not just random across the student ability range. Here is how it works.

Look at item 1 in Exhibit 10.1. For this test, there were sixty-five students in the class. If we put the data into the formula, we get

$$\text{Standard error} = \frac{1}{\sqrt{(65-1)}} = .12$$

The rule is that any correlation larger than two times the standard error will be accepted as other than a chance relationship between the item and the total score. On the basis of this criterion, we should take a serious look at item 1 in Exhibit 10.1. The correlation of item 1 with the total test score is .25; two times the standard error is .24. These statistics show item 1 to be very marginal, but acceptable by this criterion.

When instructors find a nonfunctioning item, what should they do with it? Some items can be salvaged by rereading them and noting an error in construction that can be repaired. At the time an item is written, instructors often have only one point of view in mind. After a period of time passes, or after discussing it with the class, they see there is another angle in the item that they did not at first notice. Items of this type can be revised and often salvaged for the item pool.

Items that do not fare well in item analysis need not necessarily be eliminated. They often can be revised and used again in the next testing over this unit. However, after scrutinizing an item and finding obvious problems that do not appear to be repairable, instructors may wish to eliminate the item from the pool and construct an entirely new one that covers the same topic in the table of specifications as the discarded item.

The following section deals with item analysis done by hand. Those instructors who have access to electronic scoring will probably want to skip this section.

Item Analysis by Hand

When doing an item analysis by hand, we first calculate a figure called the item *discrimination index*. To do this, we begin by putting the students' papers into order of how they scored on the tests, that is, the highest scorer first, the next highest second, and so on. Then we divide the papers in half, making one pile of high scorers and one of low scorers. These two groups represent the students who knew the course topic well and those who knew it less well.

Now look at test item 1 in the data below. In the pile of high scorers, for each option—A, B, C, and D—tabulate the number of people who chose it. Now do the same for the low scorers, and record these data. You will have a table that looks like this (* identifies the correct answer):

Item 1	Option				
	A	B	C	D*	Total
High scorers	2	4	0	16	22
Low scorers	12	7	0	4	23

Now subtract the number of correct answers for the low scorers from the number of correct answers for the high scorers, and divide this difference by the number of students in the larger of the two (low and high scorers) groups. The formula looks like this:

$$\text{Discrimination index} = \frac{(\text{NumHigh} - \text{NumLow})}{\text{Number of students in larger group}}$$

where NumHigh = the number of students in the high group who got the item correct, and NumLow = the number of students in the low group who got the item correct.

Using the above data, where option D is the correct answer, the discrimination index is calculated as follows.

$$\text{Discrimination index} = \frac{(16 - 4)}{23} = .52$$

After the calculations for item 1 are completed, go on to item 2, and so on, until all items in the entire test are analyzed.

How do we interpret the discrimination index? Although

it is not a correlation coefficient, we deal with it in much the same way. Indices run from 0 to 1.00 and can also be negative. Any item with an index at the lower end of the scale, say .20 or lower, is suspect. These items should be scrutinized for construction problems, nonfunctioning distractors, or irrelevance to the topic being assessed.

Faculty may also wish to do the above analysis for the distractors. Instructors intend that more low scorers (on the total test) select the distractors than high scorers. If this occurs, the discrimination index will be negative. In the above data, the analysis for distractor A looks like this:

$$\text{Discrimination index} = \frac{2 - 12}{23} - .44$$

Here the negative sign means that the low scorers on the total test selected the option more often than did the high scorers. We do not have to calculate an index to tell this, of course. Our reading of the data show that. But the index puts this option on the same scale as the correct answer, and the same criterion of magnitude applies in deciding if the index is an important value to consider.

If the above procedure seems to involve too much arithmetic, a simpler procedure may be carried out that is almost as useful as the above index. It is the *straight difference* method. Put the student papers into high- and low-scoring groups as before. Next, as before, for each item, tabulate the number of students in the high and low groups that select the correct option. Then simply subtract the number of correct answers in the low group from the number of correct answers in the high group. If this difference is equal to or greater than .10 times the total number in the class, the item is accepted as adequate.

Here is an example with only three options (the right answer is shown with an asterisk).

	Options		
	A	B*	C
Number in high group	8	12	5
Number in low group	10	8	7

Since B is the correct answer, we begin by subtracting eight from twelve. Then we assess this value by our criterion of .10 times the total number of students. There are fifty students in the class, so our criterion value is five. This item does not reach the criterion, so we will want to scrutinize it very carefully. The straight difference procedure eliminates the step in which we divide the difference between high and low groups by the number of students in one group. Instead, we calculate one criterion value (.10 times the total number of students) and use that value across all items.

How does the hand tabulation method based on differences compare with the computer method based on item to total test correlations? Research shows that the two methods agree very closely in terms of the extent to which they identify discriminating items. The availability of an electronic system to do the work will dictate the choice of one method over another.

Item Difficulty

The difficulty index is simply the proportion of students who get an item correct. If for a given item, twenty students out of a class of forty-five choose the correct option, the difficulty index is

$$\text{Difficulty} = 20/45 = .44$$

Difficulty indices run from 0 to 1.00. The larger the index the easier the item; the smaller the index the more difficult the item. An item that has a difficulty of .44 (like the one above) would be regarded as one that has an acceptable difficulty level. Test items should have difficulties in the vicinity of .50, because at this level the best discrimination values are obtained. It is hard to get a good discrimination index if almost everyone gets the item correct or almost everyone misses the item. The students are too "bunched up" on the item to sort them out in terms of total test performance.

Because we want the highest discrimination values we can get, and because we realize that discrimination is tied to item difficulty, we recommend that an item be regarded as most useful if it has a difficulty index in the range of .30 to .70. This does not, of course, rule out items outside this range. But items with difficulty in the above range lay the foundation for the best discrimination between the "know-its" and the "don't know-its." The final decision on whether or not to use an item, however, should be tied to both the discrimination index and the difficulty level for the item.

Analysis of Distractors

An item analysis will also indicate how well the distractors worked. Let us look at data from a hand tabulation:

	Options			
	A	B*	C	D
Number in high group	4	13	0	3
Number in low group	7	9	0	4

or data for the same item on a computer item analysis.

	A	B*	C	D
$p =$	27.5	55.0	0.0	18.5

Because distractor C was not chosen by any student, the item essentially operated as a three-option item. In this case, where we thought the chance level of guessing the item correctly was .25 (1 in 4), it was actually .33 (1 in 3), because no one was "fooled" by option C. The instructor should look carefully at the nondiscriminating option to see why it did not work. If a reason is obvious, the instructor should rewrite the option before it is put into the item bank. However, if the instructor cannot decide why the option was unattractive to some of the students, it should probably be discarded and a completely new option written.

There is another feature of distractors to look for in an item analysis. In good items, each of the distractors will be chosen more often by the low scorers than by the high scorers.

Students who do not know the material well are likely to be beguiled by wrong answers more often than persons who know the material better. In very good items, the analysis data should show this to be true for every distractor. If we do not get this result on a given distractor, we should ask why the persons who do best on the total test seem to find that distractor so interesting, while persons who know less do not find it very attractive. This is not a major feature of an item analysis, but it is an additional detail we may use to sharpen our item writing skills.

Item Response Theory and Item Analysis

Psychometricians are currently developing a number of test operations based on a psychomathematical development known variously as item response theory, latent trait theory, or item characteristics curve theory. The most commmonly used variation of this set of procedures is probably the Rasch model, named after Georg Rasch, a Danish mathematician.

Item response theory presents a very attractive item analysis procedure that is in use on an increasing scale. It calculates the odds of getting an item right and then converts this number to a natural logarithm. Item response theory procedure provides a test-equating system that allows faculty to equate the item difficulty scale on one test to the scale of another test. If classes are large, faculty can administer test A to their 10:00 A.M. section of Mathematics 101, and test B (which contains items most of which are different from test A) to their 2:00 P.M. section, and put the items of the afternoon section on the same difficulty scale as the morning section, even though neither the students nor the item sets (for the most part) are the same.

Because item response theory allows faculty to equate different item sets across different student groups, it is an especially useful system for establishing item difficulties when faculty are building item banks. Instructors want to feed new items into their item banks until they have a very large pool of items from which they may draw to build a test at any given time. When they do this, faculty must believe that all items in the pool have difficulties on the same scale. If so, faculty can even tailor the test to a given difficulty level. If all items have difficulties based on the same scale, faculty can select items that are in the difficulty range of interest.

Item Analysis for Essay Tests

Item analysis is not just for objective tests but can also be applied to essay questions. A procedure proposed by Whitney and Sabers (1970) can determine the difficulty (diff.) and discrimination (disc.) of essay questions.

Identify the upper and lower 25 percent of the students on the test. For *each* question, compute the sum of the scores for the upper 25 percent (the "highs") and the sum of scores for the bottom 25 percent (the "lows"). Apply the following formulas:

$$\text{Disc.} = \frac{(\text{sum of scores for "highs"} - \text{sum of scores for "lows"})}{N \times (\text{max. possible score on item})}$$

$$\text{Diff.} = \frac{(\text{sum of scores for "highs"} + \text{sum of scores for "lows"})}{2N \times (\text{max. possible score on item})}$$

where N = 25 percent of the number tested. Table 10.1 gives the score results for high and low groups for an essay item.

Table 10.1. Score Breakdown for an Essay Item in a History Test.

	High Group		Low Group	
Scores on Item	No. of Students	No. Students × Score	No. of Students	No. Students × Score
10	9	90	1	10
8	6	48	0	0
6	2	12	4	24
4	3	12	7	28
2	0	0	8	16
	20	162	20	78

We see that nine from the high group got the highest score (10), while only one from the low group got this highest score. If we continue in this way, we find that the sum of the scores for the high group on this item is 162; the sum of scores for the low group is 78. Now N is equal to 20 (25 percent of eighty students), and the highest possible score is 10. Substituting these values into the above formulas, we have:

$$\text{Discrimination} = (162 - 78)/200 = .42$$

and

$$\text{Difficulty} = (162 + 78)/400 = .60$$

This item has satisfactory discrimination and difficulty. Although this procedure is somewhat laborious, occasional application of these procedures will be helpful to instructors who want some data on how well their essay items are working.

Summary

Item analysis tells faculty whether their items are separating students who tend to score well on the test from those who tend to score less well. This characteristic is called item discrimination. In a computer analysis, it is shown by a point biserial correlation coefficient and, in a hand-calculated analysis, by an index of discrimination.

Item analysis also tells faculty how difficult an item is. Difficulty is shown by the proportion of people who get an item correct. The larger the index of difficulty, the more people got the item correct, and the easier the item was. Items that are too difficult, or too easy, for students will have a hard time discriminating between knowledgeable and less knowledgeable students.

By alerting instructors to nonfunctioning distractors as well as poor items overall, item analysis will help instructors revise items and thus become better item writers, a skill in which all faculty will be interested.

11

Grading

Assigning grades to students at the end of each semester is certainly one of the least pleasant aspects of college teaching. Faculty not only dislike the drudgery involved in maintaining records and calculating final grades, but they also have concerns about whether they are doing a good job of grading. Instructors often are not quite sure that their assessment of student performance has been accurate, that the assessment sampled the subject matter adequately, or that their method of grading has been equally fair to all students.

While millions of grades are assigned by faculty at the end of each semester, college professors certainly do not agree on the value of grades. Some even advocate that grades be abandoned. They point out that preoccupation with grades creates needless anxiety that may actually interfere with students' learning. Other faculty believe that grading is a well-established and important part of the educational process. They believe grades are indispensable for motivating and differentiating between students. Most faculty are somewhere in between these two extremes; they recognize the benefits but feel that grades are overemphasized.

Benefits of Grades

Grades provide the following important benefits to students.

Motivation

Grades do motivate students to study. Some students might study without tests and grades, but most probably would not put forth the effort to master subject materials without this extrinsic motivation. Eison and Pollio (1989) surveyed 1,300 faculty from colleges and universities across the country. They report that from 60 to 65 percent of faculty agree or strongly agree with the statement, "I think it useful to use grades as incentives to increase student performance." Research involving comparisons of graded versus nongraded courses (pass-fail, for example) consistently shows that achievement is higher when students know they are going to be graded. Eison and Pollio find that of the 5,000 undergraduates surveyed, 44 to 59 percent say, "without regularly scheduled exams, I would not learn and remember very much." If grades motivate students to study, then the result is that they will learn and discover the joys of learning and achievement at the same time. Ebel (1979a) points out that there is nothing wrong with encouraging students to work for high marks, if the marks are valid indications of educational achievement. He says that if there is not a close relationship between grades and achievement, then the fault lies with those who teach and assign the marks, not with the system.

Feedback

An important means of communicating, grades provide information to students about their level of achievement in particular courses, and thus grades are important to the process of intellectual self-evaluation that occurs in college. Students use grades to shed light on their strengths and weaknesses in different disciplines and to make realistic choices about majors, graduate school, and careers. A student who gets a low grade in freshman math courses would probably not want to consider majoring in physics or engineering. In a study conducted at Williams College and eight other colleges and universities, Sabot and Wakeman-Linn (1991) find that the grade received in an introductory course has a powerful effect on whether a student takes another course in the subject, regardless of initial motivation and skill. Their research shows that over the past twenty-five years, many universities have split into high- and low-grading departments, and this split has affected enrollment in the low-grading departments such as economics, mathematics, and chemistry. Sabot and Wakeman-Linn used a statistical simulation and conclude that if the mathematics department (low-grading) adopted the grading policy of the English department (high-grading) for its introductory course, 80 percent more students would take at least one more math course.

Grades also allow institutions to discriminate between students' performance, which provides the basis for determining whether students have achieved at a level to justify receiving a college degree, graduating with honors, or being admitted to graduate school. Because grades are so important to students, instructors must be fair and objective in their evaluations.

Disadvantages of Grades

Students often become so motivated by grades that they are more concerned with boosting their grade point average than with learning. Students often refrain from taking courses in unfamiliar fields or from taking advanced seminars and colloquia out of a fear of getting low grades. They feel they must stick to courses in which they are sure of getting good grades, because the grade point average figures so prominently in admission to graduate school and in job recruiting. In a recent survey at colleges and universities across the country, faculty members report that more than ever, students are anxious to earn good grades and avoid unnecessary risks. They say that today's students are worrying about graduate school and careers earlier than in previous years, some as soon as their freshman year. One student said, "Everyone thinks they have to have a certain grade-point average and test scores to get what they want. They're just burned out by the end" (Dodge, 1990, p. A33).

Students often report that preoccupation with grades disrupts their learning. For example, Becker (1968, p. 60) quotes a student leader who has very high grades:

The grading systems are so cockeyed around here you can't tell what's going on. One guy does it this way and another guy does it that way and, as I say, in a lot of these courses the only thing you can do is get in there and memorize a lot of facts. I've done that myself. I've gone into classes where that's all you could do is memorize . . . memorize and memorize. And then you go in to take the final and you put it all down on the paper, everything you've memorized, and then you forget it. You walk out of the class and your mind is purged. Perfectly clean. There's nothing in it. Someone asks you the next week what you learned in the class and you couldn't tell them anything because you didn't learn anything.

A few colleges, such as Hampshire in Massachusetts and Evergreen State in Washington, have eliminated letter grades (Dure, 1990). The schools give written evaluations of students' work instead of grades. No data are available on how employers or other institutions have reacted to the lack of letter grades.

While we can debate the advantages and disadvantages of grades, we know that grades are not going to be dispensed with in most universities. Instructors must learn to live with the system and try to make their grading as fair and accurate as possible.

Characteristics of a Good Grading System

1. Instructors should have specific and intellectually justifiable criteria for awarding grades, and they should inform students at the beginning of the course about these criteria and the grading method that will be used. Having specific criteria for grades reduces students' anxiety about what is expected and assures them that their grades will not be determined by some capricious method. If students are told the criteria for the various grades, they are much more likely to perceive an instructor's grading system as fair. Students believe that fair and explicit

grading policies are an important aspect of quality instruction, and they take the grading system into consideration when evaluating instructors.

Students should know the number of tests and the relative weight each is to receive, the various assignments that will be graded and their weight, and the method used to calculate final grades. The syllabus handed out on the first day of class is an excellent place to describe the grading system to be used in the class. The grading plan that has been announced at the beginning should be followed consistently. In the event that a change must be made because of time constraints or other unforeseen circumstances, instructors should do so only after careful consideration and after a complete explanation of the change to the students. Students complain that instructors often do not use the grading procedure that they indicated they would use. Students are justified in perceiving this practice as unfair.

2. Because the main purpose of grades is to communicate the extent to which students have learned the course material, grades should be based primarily on the students' performance on exams, quizzes, papers, and other measures of learning specified at the beginning of the course. Many professors like to consider factors such as the students' effort, interest, attitudes, improvement, class participation, and attendance as part of the course grade. Writers in the measurement field (Gronlund, 1990; Mehrens and Lehmann, 1991) advise against including these kinds of student behaviors because they contaminate the grade as a measure of achievement of the course objectives. Such admonitions are not new. Over 120 years ago, Harvard issued a statement to faculty that grades were to be assigned on the basis of academic achievement only, and no deductions were to be made because of absence, tardiness, and other forms of student misconduct (Milton, Pollio, and Eison, 1986).

There are several reasons for not including the instructor's subjective judgments of these behaviors in the grade. Factors included in a course grade should represent specific educational objectives for which faculty have provided specific instruction. Faculty do not usually provide instruction for the development or improvement of attitude, effort, and class participation; hence, the behaviors should not be part of the grade. Furthermore, if these factors are included, interpretation of the grade is very difficult. A grade will not mean the same thing for any two students, and students' transcripts do not explain how much of the grade represents achievement, and how much is due to the student's attitude, effort, interest, and so on.

Take participation as an example. The extent of class participation often depends on the student's personality. The extroverted students speak out in class, while the shy or introverted students do not. It does not seem fair to grade students on the basis of their personality traits. There are also cultural differences among today's college population that influence students' readiness to participate in class discussions. It might be easier for the instructor who wants to grade class participation to assign oral reports rather than try to evaluate the students' contributions in give-and-take discussions.

The record keeping also presents a problem. Do professors try to make notes in class on students' participation, do they depend on a good memory and do it after class, or do they keep records at all? Professors need a systematic way to categorize the qualities of this variable if it is to be included in the course grade. Frequency of responding is not enough. Some students will participate freely, but they do not say anything very worthwhile.

Similar problems are encountered when faculty try to include effort in the class grade. How does an instructor validly and reliably evaluate how much effort a particular student has made? Other students may have made just as much effort, but it was not as obvious to the instructor. And effort may not be highly correlated with achievement in the course.

If the development of communication skills is one of the objectives of the course, however, then the instructor would use class participation as a way to teach these skills. In this case, the instructor teaches students how to participate, and thus could use a measure of students' performance in class in the final grade. Actually, such behaviors as class participation and effort are most often used as "fudge factors" to change a good student's grade from, say, a B + to an A − , or an unpleasant student's grade from a B – to a C. This practice is not an objective grading procedure, because all students are not being treated equally.

An A grade should indicate that a student has an excellent grasp of the content and has achieved the course objectives to the highest extent. It should not be given to the hard-working student who has displayed a good attitude and a pleasant personality but who has only marginal achievement. Neither should a grade of C be given to the unpleasant, argumentative student who attends class irregularly but who has above-average achievement on the objective measures. It is best to let course grades reflect pure achievement of course objectives, or else they will lose meaning for those who interpret grades to evaluate students for further education or employment.

3. Grades should be based on sufficient data to permit the instructor to make valid evaluations of student achievement. For instance, one final examination is not enough to provide a picture of student achievement in a course. If the one test did not adequately sample all the course content, or if some students were having an off day and not performing typically, then the test is not a valid indicator of their achievement or a fair basis for assigning a grade. There should be a number of tests or quizzes as well as other types of assignments such as papers, projects, oral presentations, and homework problems. The greater the number and variety of assignments used to determine grades, the more valid and reliable the grades will be.

4. The data (test and exam scores) collected for grading purposes should be recorded in *quantitative* form, not as converted letter marks. Papers, homework, or classroom performance used for evaluating student achievement should also be scored using a quantitative rating system. Working with numbers contributes to greater accuracy when calculating final grades. Too much information is lost when a range of scores, some higher, others lower, is converted to the same letter grade, and this information is not likely to be retrieved when the letter grades are changed back to numbers for averaging. For example, assume an instructor gave three tests with a total of 60 possible points on each, with the A category equal to 55–60. A student received 54(B) on test 1, 53(B) on test 2, and 58(A) on test 3. By averaging

letter grades $((3 + 3 + 4)/3 = 3.3)$, the student would receive a B for the semester. If the instructor had recorded raw scores, however, the student would have a total of 165 points, or an average of 55, and would most likely receive an A for the semester.

5. The grading system should be equitable and fairly applied. The same products and standards of quality should be used for *all* students in the class. We do not recommend extra-credit work for only some students, because it changes the nature of the course requirements common to all students. Some students will ask to write a paper, for example, to raise their grades. If instructors granted this option to one student, they would have to do it for all. The extra-credit work that students propose oftentimes does not contribute to their learning of the course material. It is much wiser if students try to determine why they are not doing better on the course exams and then take corrective steps.

Of course, instructors may plan some worthwhile optional activities and announce their availability to *all* interested students at the beginning of the course. If students wish to participate, instructors may give a few extra points. But, generally, students must "run the same race" if instructors are to compare their achievement for grading purposes.

6. The basis for the grading should be statistically sound. If instructors have told students that the final exam will count 25 percent of the course grade, then they should use a procedure for combining scores that will ensure that the final exam does count 25 percent, and neither more nor less.

Assigning Grades on Examinations

Before instructors assign course grades, however, they must assign examination grades. We now look, therefore, at the two most commonly used procedures for assigning grades to a distribution of test scores.

Performance Relative to the Group

Performance relative to the group is a norm-referenced system with which most faculty are familiar. In this system, the scores are ranked from highest to lowest; the grades students receive depend on their relative ranking in the total group. If students rank at or near the top of the group, they will receive an A; students who rank lower in the group will receive letter grades of B, C, D, or F, depending on their position in the group and where the lines are drawn for the grading categories.

The question is where to draw the lines for the A's, B's, C's, and so on. There is no generally accepted "ideal" grade distribution, and the percentage of students assigned each grade may be based on an instructor's own preference. There are great differences between professors in the percentage of A's, B's, and other grades that they give in their classes; some are easy graders, while others are more severe. Departmental policy may influence the percentage of students assigned each grade. For example, a sociology department might specify that the distributions for the large introductory courses should be as follows: A = 10 percent of the students, B = 30 percent, C = 45 percent, D = 10 percent, and F = 5 percent. The percentage assigned to each grade category might be different for intermediate or advanced courses. Other departments might have a quite different grade distribution for their introductory and advanced courses. Sabot and Wakeman-Linn (1991), in their research at Williams College, find that the average grade in introductory humanities and social science courses is 3.09 on a scale of 4, while the average grade in economics, mathematics, and chemistry is 2.66.

In a norm-referenced system, the examination scores are arranged in order from high to low, and the top, say, 10 percent are assigned an A, the next 30 percent a B, and so on, according to the system to be followed. This procedure is *not* the same as the old "grading on the normal curve" system, where equal numbers of high and low grades were rigidly assigned in every course. Grading on the curve is not used very frequently anymore, because faculty know that the achievement of college students is not likely to be normally distributed.

One common norm-referenced procedure involves a visual inspection of the scores to locate breaks in the distribution, that is, several consecutive scores that no students received. These breaks are used as the dividing lines between the various grade categories. The instructor lists the scores from high to low and then separates the scores into the desired number of clusters and assigns a grade to each cluster. For example, consider the following score distribution:

	Score		Score
	83		60
	80		59
A	79	C	58
	78		52
	76		51
	71		46
	70	D	45
B	69		44
	67		
	66		

The instructor may decide to use the gaps in the distribution as the dividing points between the grade categories. Students receiving a score of 83–76 would get an A, but the student who scores 71 would get a B. Although convenient, we do not recommend this procedure, because the grade distribution depends on a judgment made after the scores are available instead of an established rule that students are familiar with prior to the testing. Also, the size and location of the gaps may be the result of random measurement errors instead of actual differences in achievement between students. An equivalent distribution of scores for the students might have the breaks at different locations or of different sizes. If this method is used, it should be restricted to score distributions that are highly variable. If the group is homogeneous, the method may contain so much error that it is unfair to some students.

Another widely used norm-referenced system employs the mean (or median) and the standard deviation to determine the different grade categories. This method works best for a class of at least twenty students. The steps are as follows:

1. Put the test scores into a frequency distribution and calculate the mean, median, and standard deviation of the scores.

Most printouts from scoring machines will have these statistics.

2. If the mean and median are close in value (within 1 point), use the mean for further calculations; otherwise, use the median. Add one-half of the standard deviation to the mean or median, and subtract one-half of the standard deviation from the mean or median. These two values will set off the C category.

3. Add one standard deviation to the upper cutoff of the C's to arrive at the upper cutoff for the B's. Subtract one standard deviation from the lower cutoff of the C's to find the cutoff for the D's.

4. Those scores beyond the B cutoff (>1.5 standard deviations) will receive A's; those beyond -1.5 standard deviations will receive F's.

The instructor can use other standard deviation units to mark off the grade categories. If the instructor believes it is a superior class, then the procedure should start with the average grade being a B instead of a C as above.

One objection to norm-referenced grading in general is that the level of performance of the class is determined by the students. The highest-scoring students will receive A's, even if their achievement is not outstanding. This type of grading also promotes competitiveness between students instead of cooperation and group study. Since only a certain number of the highest scorers will receive an A, it is not in the best interests of students to help classmates. One might also expect that norm-referenced grading has a more positive effect on the learning and motivation of those students who consistently score at or near the top of a class, while having a negative impact on those students regularly at the bottom. Some research suggests that norm-referenced grading may in fact have a differential effect on students (Natriello, 1987). It may diminish low-scoring students' motivation and their perceptions of their academic ability but encourage the top students. In norm-referenced grading, a student's grade is a result not only of that individual's achievement but also of the achievement of others in the class. Students in class sections having many low-achieving students can more easily get a good grade than can students in higher-achieving sections. In large, nonselective lecture courses enrolling several hundred students, instructors can feel more confident that the class group is representative of the population of students and can assign grades using the total group as the reference point. But with small sections (30 to 40 students), the section-to-section differences in ability may result in sampling error that could make as much as a one-grade difference for a number of students. To use a norm-referenced system, the distribution of grades should be flexible enough to allow for variation in the caliber of students from one section or one course to another. Instructors teaching small classes should modify the allocation of grades to take into account the ability level of the group.

Anchoring

To overcome the instability of small size classes, instructors can use *anchoring* (Hanna and Cashin, 1988). An anchor measure is a device that instructors use to judge or gauge the ability status of a class. If instructors have taught a class several times and have used the same or an equivalent exam, then the distribution of test scores accumulated over many classes can serve as the anchor. The present class is compared with this cumulative distribution to judge the ability level of the group and the appropriate allocation of grades. Anchoring also works well in multisection courses where the same text, same syllabus, and same examinations are used. The common examination can be used to reveal whether and how the class groups differ in achievement, and the grade distributions in the individual sections can be adjusted accordingly. The overall distribution of all sections serves as the anchor measure because it is relevant and large enough to provide a stable reference point. Exhibit 11.1 illustrates the concept of anchoring.

Assume that departmental policy states that in typical sections there will be 15 percent A, 25 percent B, 40 percent C, 15 percent D, and 5 percent F. If we apply this rule to the large distribution at the left in Exhibit 11.1, we can identify the scores corresponding to the various grade categories. Each instructor

Exhibit 11.1. Example of the Use of a Total Distribution as Anchor.

	Cumulative Distribution for Many Sections ($N = 500$)			Professor X's Section ($N = 35$)	
	Score	Frequency		Score	Frequency
	85	2		85	1
	84	2		83	3
	83	4	A	82	1
	82	4		80	2
A	81	12		79	3
	80	12		77	1
	79	14		75	4
	78	16		74	2
	77	8		73	1
	76	26	B	69	5
	75	12		68	3
	74	8		67	2
	73	14		65	1
B	72	10	C	64	2
	71	14		63	2
	70	16		60	2
	69	6			
	68	4			
	67	2			
	66	14			
	65	34			
	64	28			
	63	24			
	62	20			
	61	16			
C	60	18			
	59	12			
	58	14			
	57	6			
	56	10			
	55	10			
	54	8			
	53	10			
	52	12			
	51	12			
	50	8			
D	49	10			
	48	6			
	47	8			
	46	6			
	45	2			
	44	2			
	43	12			
F	42	8			
	41	2			
	40	2			

teaching this multisection course can then compare his or her section to the overall distribution and grade accordingly. Professor X's section, whose scores are shown at the right in Exhibit 11.1, appears to be an above-average group. Thirty-two percent of the students are in the 77–85, or A, category; almost half (49 percent) fall in the 66–76, or B, category; and the remaining 20 percent will receive C's. There are no D or F students in this section. Using the large, more stable distribution as an anchor avoids the problem of trying to force the departmental grading policy on a section that is not typical.

If an instructor is teaching a class for the first time and has no other scores for comparison, a relevant and well-constructed teacher-made pretest may be used as an anchor. For example, a pretest covering basic statistical concepts could provide a basis for anchoring an advanced statistics class. Or a French instructor could use a test of French grammar and reading to gauge the ability level of a class.

Performance Relative to a Standard

In performance relative to a standard, also known as criterion-referenced grading, students' grades are determined by comparing their overall point total with a standard set by the instructor. The standard is most commonly the percentage of the total possible points on the examination. Grades are then defined by some percentage-correct range: for example, A = 95–100 percent of the total possible points, A − = 90–94 percent, B + = 88–89 percent, and so on. There is no curve or predetermined distribution of grades. The standards are absolute, and every student can get an A, or every student can get a C, depending on where their overall point total falls with respect to the standard.

In this type of grading, the scores depend on the difficulty of the test. Instructors can develop a test on which none of the students achieve, say, 80 percent of the possible points. Or they can develop a test on which most students get at least 90 percent of the items correct. What happens when the highest score obtained on an exam is only 70 percent? Instructors often try to make adjustments if scores turn out to be too low. They may give everyone so many percentage points, or they make the next test very easy to compensate for the difficult test. Occasionally, they follow the questionable procedure of making the top score in the class (say, 70 percent of the maximum) an A, even though it does not meet the absolute standard for an A. Because of this disadvantage, criterion-referenced scoring is not as popular in college classes as some type of norm-referenced grading.

Another way instructors can utilize criterion-referenced grading is by making a list of objectives that are required for each grade level. If students achieve them all successfully, they receive A's. Other grades are given according to the extent to which the objectives are attained. For example, to receive an A in a course, the student may be required to write three acceptable papers and make a 95 percent passing score on each of twelve unit tests. A grade of B might require two acceptable papers and at least an 85 percent score on ten unit tests, and so on. Each student's performance is observed and evaluated independently of the performance of others. With criterion-referenced grading, there may be a high percentage of A's in a class if students master the content and objectives required for that grade. Some researchers who have studied the above type of mastery learning (Harris and Liguori, 1974) find that it produces an inordinate number of A's and B's and also a large number of incompletes and withdrawals. Harris and Liguori suggest that the number of high marks and the leniency in completing courses may fail to prepare students for performance in later course work.

Assigning Course Grades

After instructors collect the individual graded components (exams, quizzes, and papers), they must combine them into a composite score that serves as the basis for the final course grade. Each of the components will carry more or less weight in the composite. How much weight is given to each of the components in the final grade depends on the nature and objectives of the course and the importance of the measures to those objectives. A grade in English composition may be determined almost entirely by papers; a grade in chemistry by exams and lab projects; a grade in physical education by exams and ratings of performance. The more important the component is to the objectives of the course, the greater the weight it should receive in the final grade. An exam should be weighted more heavily than a quiz, for example, and an exam that covers more material or more difficult material should be weighted more heavily than exams covering less material and requiring less preparation.

Weighting Scores

How do instructors combine data into a composite score so that the various components carry the appropriate weight? In a norm-referenced system, the actual weight that a component carries depends on the variability, or spread, of scores on that measure. If the variability is not considered, the relative weight of the components will likely be different from those that the instructor announced to students. Although a number of components should be weighted in a final grade, we will illustrate this process by assuming that only a final exam and a paper are used, each receiving equal weight. The range on the exam was 20 points (90–70), while the range on the paper was 40 points (50–10). Note that the relative performance of the two students on the exam is exactly opposite their performance on the paper.

	Exam	*Scores* Paper	Total
Mary	90	10	100
John	70	50	120
Maximum score	90	50	
Average	80	30	
Range	20	40	

Mary is highest on the exam and lowest on the paper, while John is lowest on the exam and highest on the paper. If these two components had been weighted equally in the composite, the relative standing of the two students would be equal. But the ranking of the total score is affected more by the paper than by the exam, so simply adding the scores from the two measures does not give equal representation. Scores on the paper actually have twice the weight in determining the final ranking of students because the score variability (range) of the paper was twice that of the exam. The two measures can be given equal weight by multiplying by a factor that makes the two score ranges equal, that is, by multiplying each exam score by two. After multiplying, Mary would have a composite score of 190 (180 + 10), and John would also have a score of 190 (140 + 50). If the instructor wanted the final exam to count twice as much as the paper, it would be necessary to multiply each exam score by four.

A more precise weighting system uses the standard deviation of the scores rather than the range as the measure of variability. Standard deviation is preferred because it reflects the variability among *all* the scores, whereas the range depends on the values of only the highest and lowest scores. Adding some points to the highest score could change the range considerably even though the variability of all other scores remains unchanged. Procedures for calculating the standard deviation are discussed in any introductory statistics textbook, and it is one of the statistics typically provided faculty who use machine scoring.

Another way to insure proper weighting of the components in a composite score is to convert all scores to a standard such as a T score (mean of 50, standard deviation of 10). When converted to standard scores, all sets of scores have the same mean and standard deviation. Because the standard deviations are equal, instructors can easily apply the desired weights to the different components. Most computerized scoring systems provide instructors with T scores along with the raw scores.

The desired weight can thus be obtained by simply multiplying each standard score by the weight. Consider the following example:

	Raw Score	Student T score	Desired Weight	Weighted Score
Midterm	88	75	1	75
Final	75	65	2	130
Paper	50	60	1	60
		Composite Score		265

In this example, the instructor wants the final exam to have twice the weight of the midterm and the paper, so the final exam scores are multiplied by two. The composite T score can be divided by the sum of the weights (in this case four) to obtain a composite average for each student. Once each student has either a total composite score or a composite average, the instructor can put the numbered scores into a distribution and use one of the previously discussed procedures to convert the numbers into letter grades for the course.

Weighting is easy if instructors remember that the weight of one measure relative to others is proportional to the variability of the respective measures. Procedures that should *not* be used to weight include increasing the length of the test that is to be more heavily weighted. An eighty-item test will not necessarily have twice the weight of a forty-item test if we add scores from the two tests together. Also, one test cannot be made to count twice as much as another simply by doubling the scores on the first test and then adding the two together. In the first example above, we could not make the exam count twice as much as the paper by doubling the exam scores. Each exam score would have to be multiplied by four if we wanted the exam to count twice as much as the paper.

Grading by Computer

Most universities provide computerized grade book programs to their faculty. These programs, which run on mainframe computers, accumulate scores from tests, quizzes, and other grade components, weight them differentially as directed, and produce a final course composite and grade. Although the computerized grade books are designed to be used with optically scanned answer sheets, other data such as essay test scores and laboratory report grades can be added. Some programs permit students to access the records to see how they are doing in the course. Computerized records keeping is especially helpful with large classes.

There are also many computer-grading programs on the market that are designed for professors' personal computers.

Professors themselves can enter students' numerical data on the various grading components, or, if they have tests optically scanned, they can request that the data be put on a disk ready for analysis on their own computers.

Other Systems for Assigning Grades

There are other grading systems available to instructors.

Contract Grading

In contract grading, the students and the instructor arrive at an agreement on what needs to be done to receive a certain grade. Generally, the professor lists a variety of objectives or activities that students can achieve or participate in to earn points in the course. Criteria of quality as well as quantity should be specified. Students select those objectives that will give them the grade they want and sign a written contract with the professor. This is done early in the course, usually within the first week. Participation by the student in establishing a contract should minimize later complaints about the unfairness of a course grade.

Exhibits 11.2 and 11.3 are examples of contracts based on a point system and an activity system (Fuhrmann and Grasha, 1983).

Self-Assessment

Self-assessment is a method that has been receiving more attention in recent years. It is based on the assumption that because learning is a lifelong process, students should learn not only to work independently but also to assess their own progress and performance. A number of writers in higher education are advocating that faculty give students more opportunities to assess their own learning because it is a skill that will be helpful when students enter the working world. Self-assessment has not been used widely, however, because most faculty fear that students cannot be objective in assessing their own achievement.

Exhibit 11.2. Components of a Point Contract System.

Activity	Points Earned
Exams	
90–100 items correct	50 points each exam
80–89 items correct	40 points each exam
70–79 items correct	30 points each exam
0–69 items correct	0 points each exam
Design a research project.	20 points
Implement a research project.	40 points
Write a book report on as many outside reading books as you want.	30 points each report
Run a class session on a topic of choice related to course content.	35 points
Take a field trip and write a report on your observations.	30 points each report
Write a term paper.	60 points
Classroom attendance.	3 points each class
Negotiate with the instructor one or more projects of interest to you.	Variable points
Points needed for a grade.	A = 350+ B = 275–349
	C = 200–274 No D or F

I have read the requirements for earning points toward a grade in this course. I would like to contract for a _____ grade by earning a minimum of _____ points. The activities I have elected to do to earn points are the following (list activities and corresponding points on a separate page).

I understand that I can change my contract to try for a higher or lower grade until 15 March. This change must be approved by the instructor. All work on this contract must be done to the quality standards set by the teacher. The teacher agrees to give me feedback on a timely basis regarding the quality of all work completed.

Date: _____ Student Signature: _____
Instructor Signature: _____

Success in self-assessment has generally been measured by the extent of agreement between self- and instructor marks. An early study concludes that students are unable to assign their own grades objectively and realistically (Burke, 1969). Burke finds only 60 percent agreement between self- and instructor ratings of performance. Most students felt they deserved at least a grade of B.

More recently, Falchikov and Boud (1989) reviewed the research literature on student self-assessment in higher education.

Exhibit 11.3. Components of an Activity Contract System.

	Grade		
Activities	A	B	C
*Midterm exam	90–100%	80–89%	70–79%
*Final exam	90–100%	80–89%	70–79%
**Assignments			
Short essay questions in workbook	Complete 25	Complete 15	Complete 10
Workbook exercises	Complete 10	Complete 6	Complete 3
Outside readings with report	Read 6	Read 4	Read 2
Position papers	Write 3	Write 2	Write 1
Textbook readings	5 chapters	5 chapters	5 chapters
In-class presentations	Make 2	Make 1	None
Research project	Design and implement	Design only	None

*You may take a makeup exam to get the percentage needed if you fail to achieve it the first time. A makeup will be given only once. Failure to achieve a midterm or final exam score appropriate to your contract will result in your final grade being lowered one letter grade.
**All assignments must be completed to the standards outlined in the syllabus.

– – – – – – – – – – – – – – (tear off and turn-in) – – – – – – – – – – – – – –

Name: (last) _____ (first) _____ (mi) _____
I.D. number _____

   I have read the syllabus and understand the course requirements and the quality standards for each requirement. I have also read the criteria for an A, B, or C grade and would like to contract for a _____ grade. I understand that the instructor will give me feedback on my performance and notify me periodically whether my performance is satisfactory and in line with the requirements of the contract. Failure to meet the requirements for the grade I contracted for will lead to an appropriate lower final grade. I cannot increase or decrease the grade I contracted for without prior discussion and approval of the instructor.

Signed: _____
Date: _____

Their analysis shows that the correlations between instructor and student marks average only 0.39. Another way they express the extent of correspondence between student and faculty marks is to look at the percentages of agreement. They find that the percentages of self-assessors whose grades agree with those of faculty markers vary from 33 percent to 99.4 percent, with an average of 64.1 percent. Their research shows that students in advanced courses are more accurate assessors than students in introductory courses. That is, the marks that experienced students give their own work matches much more closely the marks assigned by their instructors. The area of study is also a factor; students within the area of science produce more accurate self-assessment than do those from other areas.

Because of the subjectivity involved in self-evaluation, we recommend that the instructor and the student meet jointly to discuss the student's achievement before any self-evaluation is made. Students will need help in going about making the evaluation—what criteria to use, and so on. How much of a role the self-evaluation should play in assigning the final grade is up to the instructor. We do not believe that self-assessment can be used as a replacement for the grading done by the instructor. Considering the competition for grades, students may not be totally honest in their self-evaluations; such a procedure could reward the dishonest student and penalize the student who tries to be honest.

Peer Grading

Peer grading is a method that has been used to evaluate students' performance in some classroom situations. Burke (1969) reports greater agreement between peer and instructor ratings (80 percent) than between self-evaluation and instructor grades (60 percent). The nature of the course is an important determinant of the usefulness and effectiveness of the method for assigning course grades. Peer grading, which should always be done anonymously, could be used to advantage in a speech class, where the instructor might have the students evaluate fellow students' oral presentations. Peer grading is also often used in English composition classes. In addition to a rating or a letter grade, students might also be asked to make specific comments on the strengths and weaknesses of the paper or presentation. If students are told what to look for and how to rate or grade, they can do a good job. Even if peer ratings are too lenient, as some professors complain, the instructor will also be grading and will have the final word.

Grading Systems

How many grading levels should be used to report grades?

Multiple Categories

Some schools use the traditional five-category system, A,B,C,D,F, but most universities now use more than the basic five categories. The most popular is a thirteen-category system, that is, A,B,C,D,F with plus and minus signs on all grades except the F. We favor the use of plus and minus signs with the five letters. Use of the signs permits instructors to differentiate levels of achievement within a broad category. For example, in Exhibit 11.1, the C category extends from 65 to 54. Under a five-category system, the person who received a 54 and just missed a D would get the same grade as the student who got a 65 and just missed the B category. As the number of grade categories increases, the frequency of errors in assigning grades may increase, but, if an error is made, it is not as crucial in its consequences as it is when there are fewer categories. It is not as serious an error if a student who perhaps earned a B receives a B – as it is if the student receives a C.

Another variation on the 5-point (A–F) grading scale combines letters to make an intermediate number of grade categories. For example, instead of pluses and minuses, some universities use the A, AB, B, BC, C, D, and F scale. This system provides for more differentiation than the five-point scale but less than the plus-minus system. It also avoids the stigma that may be attached to minus grades (Brown, 1981).

Pass-Fail

A system that became popular in the mid 1960s uses only two categories—pass or fail (P-F). It was thought that this grading system encouraged students to take courses in "academically unfamiliar" areas that they would not otherwise take because of a fear of getting a low grade. The research indicates, however, that students often use this P-F option to reduce the effort and study time in that area so they can concentrate on other courses where they are being graded. Consequently, students do not perform as well or learn as much in these P-F courses as in regularly graded courses. Pass-fail grading seems to work best in small seminars, where students are more motivated by feelings of responsibility to the instructor and the rest of the class.

Quann (1984) writes, "Interest in Pass/Fail and similar grading options appears to be waning, and institutions increasingly place restrictions on use of the non-traditional grading options" (p. 25). Some schools maintain the P-F option but will allow students to use it only in courses outside their major.

Problems in Grading

Even though instructors have used a fair and objective grading system, they may still encounter complaints from some students.

Students Who Want Grades Changed

Instructors should be willing to review grades at the request of their students. If a grade is to be useful, students must understand the reason for it. But what do instructors do about the students who come to the office and make an appeal to have their grades changed for one reason or another. Some may be good students who just missed the A they say they must have to begin study in a certain major, to get into graduate school, to graduate with honors, and so on. Others say they need a certain grade to stay eligible for athletics or just to graduate. In either case, they may try to coerce professors to give them the grade they want. The best way to deal with this situation is to refer students to the course syllabus, where the specific criteria for grades are listed, and then explain exactly how these criteria were used to arrive at their grades. Students need to understand that they *earn* grades; professors do not *give* them. Having explicit and objective criteria certainly makes it easier to justify grades.

It is best not to change a grade unless a mistake has been made in the calculations underlying it. If instructors have used a fair and objective grading system, then they must stand by their decision. If word gets around that an instructor is a soft touch who will change a grade if challenged, then he or she is likely to find the requests increasing each semester. An instructor who changes a grade when pressured is being unfair to those students who are not bold enough to challenge the instructor on the grade. Certain students should not have higher grades than they deserve simply because they are more audacious than their classmates.

Posting Grades

It has long been customary to post students' test scores or final course grades. The legality of posting grades has come into question, however, and some schools have discontinued this practice. If individual students are listed only by numbers to protect their identities, posting score or grade distributions seems to be acceptable. The posted scores are sometimes the only feedback that students receive.

Some of the newer scannable answer sheets have a consent form that students sign, indicating their agreement to have the scores posted.

Summary

The hardest part of teaching a course may be assigning the grades at the end. Grades are used to tell students how well they have achieved the objectives of the course. Grades motivate students to study and provide feedback about their relative strengths and weaknesses in various areas. However, students often become more concerned with getting grades than they do with learning.

There are a number of grading schemes available to faculty. In the widely used norm-referenced scheme, a student's grade is based on the student's performance relative to other students. In the criterion-referenced grading scheme, a student's performance is compared to a standard. Each scheme has its advantages and disadvantages. Anchoring was introduced as a way to overcome some of the disadvantages of the norm-referenced procedures. Grading policies and procedures often differ between departments within a college or university.

Whatever grading system is used, it should reflect only students' achievement of the course objectives. Using factors such as attitude, effort, participation, and attendance in determining course grades is unfair and reduces the validity of those grades.

A good grading system has certain characteristics:

1. It should be based on an adequate sampling of students' academic performance.
2. It should be equitable and fairly applied.
3. The grading system to be used should be explained at the beginning of the semester, and it should not be changed without notice to the students.
4. The various components entering into the calculation of the final grade should be weighted in terms of their relative importance.

Increasing the number of grade categories from five to thirteen by using plus and minus signs permits instructors to make finer distinctions between students. Pass-fail grading may encourage students to take courses in unfamiliar areas, but students do not work as hard or learn as much in these courses.

Other less popular approaches to grading in the college classroom are contract grading and grading by students themselves (self-assessment) and by peers.

12

Epilogue

We have written this book because we believe that (1) assessment of student achievement is one very important thing faculty members do and (2) few faculty have had any formal training in test construction and application. Instructors find themselves steeped in the knowledge, methodologies, and social role of their major discipline. They begin their careers as college professors by delivering well-prepared lectures, with audiovisual backup and reinforcing discussions. Then it comes time to see how well students are achieving the course objectives; the leap from teaching to testing is a sobering one.

This book was planned to help faculty become as skilled at testing as they are at disseminating information in their specialty. We began by presenting assessment concepts, ideas about planning a test, and theory that applies to all measurement — test reliability and validity. If a test is a consistent measure, that is, if a student's two parallel test scores agree as to the achievement of that student — we say the test is reliable. If it is not reliable, we do not know the extent to which the student's score is loaded with chance and other sources of error. If we are going to make decisions about a student's status based on achievement of course objectives, a test must carefully sample those objectives in its content. If a test does this, we say it has content validity. The themes of reliability and validity pervade the book, because no assessment procedure is workable unless we can have some confidence in its reliability and validity at the outset.

But how do instructors put reliability and validity into their tests? To do a good job of ranking students consistently (reliability) on their grasp of course objectives (validity), instructors must build good test items. For this reason, three chapters illustrate how to write various kinds of items. Instructors may not wish to use all of the item types we include, but a variety of test types can best assess the range of objectives most faculty have for their students. No test item is without its limitations, so trying out some "new" types of assessment can add to the versatility of instructors' tests and to the interest level of their students.

There is, however, more to testing than just writing items. The way a test is administered also has an impact on reliability and validity, and we have tried to point out how to administer tests well. Test scoring and reporting is an important adjunct operation, and we have discussed this. A grasp of these points will provide faculty with the essentials of basic classroom assessment.

To help instructors go beyond the essentials, we have included much additional information—how to scrutinize test items to select the ones that will sort out the capable from the not so capable students; how to use alternative assessment procedures such as portfolios, journals, and take-home tests; and how to incorporate the computer into the testing scene.

We sincerely feel by the time instructors have mastered the topics in this book, they will be far ahead of the rest of faculty in testing skill and will have found the time and effort well worthwhile. Every chapter in the book will not be equally important for everyone. However, the first three are, and we hope everyone who picks up the book will read these, because they pertain to all types of assessment, no matter what its form may be. Beyond this, we hope readers will find the entire book useful, but if an instructor wishes to begin by developing a favorite kind of test procedure, we cannot quarrel with this, but we hope you will not stop there. Our intent is that all faculty will become versatile and flexible test developers. We believe the testing techniques described will enhance instructors' professional skill and give them more confidence in their classroom procedures.

References

A Freshman Profile. Bloomington: Office of the Dean of the Faculties/Academic Affairs, Indiana University, 1991.

Aiken, L. R. "Another Look at Weighting Test Items." *Journal of Educational Measurement,* 1966, *3,* 183–185.

Aiken, L. R. "Analyzing Optional Test Items." *Educational and Psychological Measurement,* 1989, *49,* 783–787.

Anderson, S. B. "The Role of the Teacher-Made Test in Higher Education." In D. Bray and M. Belcher (eds.), *Issues in Student Assessment.* New Directions for Community Colleges, no. 59. San Francisco: Jossey-Bass, 1987.

Arter, J. A., and Spandel, V. "Using Portfolios of Student Work in Instruction and Assessment." *Educational Measurement: Issues and Practices,* 1992, *11*(1), 36–44.

Ashburn, R. R. "An Experiment in Essay-Type Questions." *Journal of Experimental Education,* 1938, *7,* 1–3.

Aubrecht, G. J. "Is There a Connection Between Testing and Teaching?" *Journal of College Science Teaching,* 1991, *20,* 152–157.

Baxter, G. P., Shavelson, R. J., Goldman, S. R., and Pine, J. "Evaluation of Procedure-Based Scoring for Hands-On Science Assessment." *Journal of Educational Measurement,* 1992, *29*(1), 1–17.

Becker, H. S., Geer, B., and Hughes, E. C. *Making the Grade: The Academic Side of College.* New York: Wiley, 1968.

Belanoff, P., and Elbow, P. "Using Portfolios to Increase Collaboration and Community in a Writing Program." *Writing Program Administration,* 1986, *9*(3), 27–40.

Bennett, R., Rock, D., and Wang, M. "Equivalence of Free-Response and Multiple-Choice Items." *Journal of Educational Measurement,* 1991, *28,* 77–92.

Ben-Shakhar, G., and Sinai, Y. "Gender Differences in Multiple-Choice Tests: The Role of Differential Guessing Tendencies." *Journal of Educational Measurement,* 1991, *28*(1), 23–35.

Blok, H. "Estimating the Reliability, Validity and Invalidity of Essay Ratings." *Journal of Educational Measurement,* 1985, *22,* 41–52.

Bloom, B. S. (ed.). *Taxonomy of Educational Objectives.* Vol. 1: *Cognitive Domain.* New York: McKay, 1956.

Boniface, D. "Candidates' Use of Notes and Textbooks During an Open-Book Examination." *Educational Research,* 1985, *27,* 201–209.

Boyer, E. *School Reform: A National Strategy.* The Carnegie Foundation for the Advancement of Teaching, Princeton: Princeton University Press, 1989.

Bracht, G. H. "The Comparative Value of Objective and Essay Testing in Undergraduate Education: Implications for Valid Assessment of Instruction." Unpublished master's thesis, University of Colorado, 1967.

Bracht, G. H., and Hopkins, K. D. "Objective and Essay Tests: Do They Measure Different Abilities?" Paper presented at the meeting of the American Educational Research Association, Chicago, April 1968.

Breland, H. M., and Gaynor, L. "A Comparison of Direct and Indirect Assessment of Writing Skills." *Journal of Educational Measurement,* 1979, *16,* 119–128.

Brown, F. G. *Measuring Classroom Achievement.* Troy, Mo.: Holt, Rinehart & Winston, 1981.

Buchanan, R. W., and Rogers, M. "Innovative Assessment in Large Classes." *College Teaching,* 1990, *38*(2), 69–73.

Burke, R. "Self-Evaluations and Peer Ratings." *Journal of Educational Research,* 1969, *62,* 444–448.

Carter, K. "Test-Wiseness for Teachers and Students." *Educational Measurement Issues and Practice*, 1986, *5*, 20–23.

Cates, W. M. "Retesting: A Logical Alternative in College Instruction." *Improving College and University Teaching*, 1984, *32*, 99–103.

Centra, J. A. *Determining Faculty Effectiveness: Assessing Teaching, Research, and Service for Personnel Decisions and Improvement*. San Francisco: Jossey-Bass, 1981.

Chase, C. I. "Impact of Some Obvious Variables on Essay-Test Scores." *Journal of Educational Measurement*, 1968, *5*, 315–318.

Chase, C. I. "Impact of Achievement Expectations and Handwriting Quality on Scoring Essay Tests." *Journal of Educational Measurement*, 1979, *16*, 39–42.

Chase, C. I. "Essay Test Scores and Reading Difficulty." *Journal of Educational Measurement*, 1983, *20*, 293–298.

Chiodo, J. J. "The Effects of Exam Anxiety on Grandma's Health." *The Chronicle of Higher Education*, Aug. 6, 1986, p. 68.

Crooks, T. J. "The Impact of Classroom Evaluation Practices on Students." *Review of Educational Research*, 1988, *58*, 438–481.

Cross, T. L. "Testing in the College Classroom." Paper presented at the annual meeting of American Educational Research Association, Boston, April 1990.

Daly, J. D., and Dickson-Markman, F. "Contrast Effects in Evaluating Essays." *Journal of Educational Measurement*, 1982, *19*, 309–316.

Davidson, W. B., House, W. J., and Boyd, T. L. "A Test-Retest Policy for Introductory Psychology Courses." *Teaching of Psychology*, 1984, *11*, 182–184.

Dempster, F. N. "Time and the Production of Classroom Learning: Discerning Implications from Basic Research." *Educational Psychologist*, 1987, *22*, 1–21.

Diamond, J., and Evans, W. "The Correction for Guessing." *Review of Educational Research*, 1973, *43*, 181–191.

Dodd, D. K., and Leal, L. "Answer Justification: Removing the 'Trick' from Multi-Choice Questions." *Teaching of Psychology*, 1988, *15*, 37–38.

Dodge, S. "Many Undergraduates Are Choosing 'Practical' Majors to Prepare for the Tough Times They Think Lie Ahead." *The Chronicle of Higher Education*, Jan. 31, 1990, p. A33.

Dure, B. "Letter Grading Gets an F." *U: The National College Newspaper.* Nov./Dec., 1990, p. 12.

D'Ydewalle, G., Swerts, A., and deCorte, E. "Study Time and Test Performance as a Function of Test Expectations." *Contemporary Educational Psychology,* 1983, *8,* 55–67.

Ebel, R. L. *Essentials of Educational Measurement.* Englewood Cliffs, N.J.: Prentice-Hall, 1965.

Ebel, R. L. "Can Teachers Write Good True-False Test Items?" *Journal of Educational Measurement,* 1975, *12,* 31–36.

Ebel, R. L. *Essentials of Educational Measurement.* (3rd ed.) Englewood Cliffs, N.J.: Prentice-Hall, 1979a.

Ebel, R. L. "Expected Reliability as a Function of Choices per Item." *Educational and Psychological Measurement,* 1979b, *29,* 565–567.

Eble, K. E. *The Craft of Teaching: A Guide to Mastering the Professor's Art.* (2nd ed.) San Francisco: Jossey-Bass, 1988.

Eison, J., and Pollio, H. R. *LOGO II: Bibliographic and Statistical Update.* Cape Girardeau: Center for Teaching and Learning, Southeast Missouri State University, 1989.

Falchikov, N., and Boud, D. "Student Self-Assessment in Higher Education: A Meta-Analysis." *Review of Educational Research,* 1989, *59,* 395–430.

Findlayson, D. S. "The Reliability of Marking of Essays." *Journal of Educational Psychology,* 1951, *21,* 126–134.

Frary, R. B. "The None-of-the-Above Option: An Empirical Study." *Applied Measurement in Education,* 1991, *4*(2), 115–124.

Friedman, H. "Immediate Feedback, No Return Test Procedure for Introductory Courses." *Teaching of Psychology,* 1987, *15,* 37–38.

Frisbie, D. A. "Multiple Choice and True-False: A Comparison of Reliability and Concurrent Validity." *Journal of Educational Measurement,* 1974, *10,* 297–304.

Frisbie, D. A. "Reliability of Scores from Teacher-Made Tests." *Educational Measurement: Issues and Practices,* 1988, *7,* 25–35.

Frisbie, D. A., and Sweeney, D. C. "The Relative Merits of Multiple True-False Achievement Tests." *Journal of Educational Measurement,* 1982, *19,* 29–35.

Fuhrmann, B., and Grasha, A. *A Practical Handbook for College Teachers.* Boston: Little, Brown, 1983.

Goodwin, S., and others. *Effective Classroom Questioning.* Urbana-Champaign: Office of Instructional and Management Services, University of Illinois, n.d.

Grant, L. D., and Caplan, N. "Studies in the Reliability of Short-Answer Examinations." *Journal of Educational Research,* 1957, *51,* 109–116.

Gribbin, W. G. "Writing Across the Curriculum: Assignments and Evaluation." *Clearing House,* 1991, *64,* 365–368.

Gronlund, N. E. *Measurement and Evaluation in Teaching.* (5th ed.) New York: Macmillan, 1985.

Gronlund, N. E. *Measurement and Evaluation in Teaching.* (6th ed.) New York: Macmillan, 1990.

Haladyna, T. M. "Context-Dependent Item Sets." *Educational Measurement: Issues and Practices,* 1992, *11*(1), 21–25.

Hanna, G. S., and Cashin, W. E. *Improving College Grading.* Idea Paper no. 19. Manhattan: Center for Faculty Evaluation and Development, Kansas State University, 1988.

Harari, H., and McDavid, J. W. "Name Stereotypes and Teachers' Expectations." *Journal of Educational Psychology,* 1973, *65,* 222–225.

Harris, M. B., and Liguori, R. A. "Some Effects of a Personalized System of Instruction in Teaching College Mathematics." *Journal of Educational Research,* 1974, *68*(2), 62–66.

Hendrickson, J. M., Brady, M. P., and Algozzine, B. "Peer-Mediated Testing: The Effects of an Alternative Testing Procedure in Higher Education." *Educational and Psychological Research,* 1987, 91–101.

Hill, K. T. "Debilitating Motivation and Testing: A Major Educational Problem." In R. E. Ames and C. Ames (eds.), *Research on Motivation in Education.* Vol. 1: *Student Motivation.* San Diego: Academic Press, 1984.

Hogan, T. P., and Mishler, C. "Relation Between Essay Tests and Objective Tests of Language Skills for Elementary School Students." *Journal of Educational Measurement,* 1980, *17,* 219–227.

Holmgren, P. "Avoiding the Exam-Return Question 'Wall'—Working with Your SERC Committee." *Journal of College Science Teaching,* 1992, *21*(4), 214–216.

Hughes, D. C., and Keeling, B. "The Use of Context Effects in Essay Scoring." *Journal of Educational Measurement,* 1984, *21,* 277–281.

224 References

James, A. W. "The Effect of Handwriting on Grading." *English Journal,* 1927, *16,* 180–205.

Jedrey, C. M. "Grading and Evaluation." In M. Gullette (ed.), *The Art and Craft of Teaching.* Cambridge: Harvard-Danforth Center for Teaching and Learning, 1982.

Jendrek, M. P. "Faculty Reactions to Academic Dishonesty." *Journal of College Student Development,* 1989, *30,* 401–406.

Kulhavy, R. W. "Feedback in Written Instruction." *Review of Educational Research,* 1977, *47,* 211–232.

Leahy, R. "The Power of the Student Journal." *College Teaching,* 1985, *33*(3), 108–112.

Lundeberg, M. A., and Fox, P. W. "Do Laboratory Findings on Test Expectancy Generalize to Classroom Outcomes?" *Review of Educational Research,* 1991, *61*(1), 94–106.

McKee, B. G., and Manning-Curtis, C. "Teacher-Constructed Classroom Tests: The Stepchild of Measurement Research." Paper presented at the annual meeting of the National Conference of Measurement in Education, New York, March 1982.

McMorris, R. F., DeMers, L. P., and Schwarz, S. P. "Attitudes, Behaviors, and Reasons for Changing Responses Following Answer-Changing Instruction." *Journal of Educational Measurement,* 1987, *24*(2), 131–143.

McMorris, R. F., Urbach, S., and Connor, M. "Effects of Incorporating Humor in Test Items." *Journal of Educational Measurement,* 1985, *22*(2), 147–155.

McMullen-Pastrick, M., and Gleason, M. "Examinations: Accentuating the Positive." *College Teaching,* 1986, *34,* 135–139.

Marshall, J. C., and Powers, J. M. "Writing Neatness, Composition Errors and Essay Grades." *Journal of Educational Measurement,* 1969, *6,* 97–101.

Marton, F., and Säljö, R. "On Qualitative Differences in Learning: Outcome and Process." *British Journal of Educational Psychology,* 1976, *46,* 115–127.

Mehrens, W. A., and Lehmann, I. J. *Measurement and Evaluation in Education and Psychology.* Troy, Mo.: Holt, Rinehart & Winston, 1991.

Mentzer, T. L. "Response Biases in Multiple-Choice Test Item Files." *Educational and Psychological Measurement,* 1982, *42,* 437–448.

Metzger, R., and others. "The Classroom as Learning Context: Changing Rooms Affects Performance." *Journal of Educational Psychology*, 1979, *71*, 440–442.

Michael, W. B., Stewart, R., Douglass, B., and Rainwater, J. H. "An Experimental Determination of the Optimal Scoring Formula for a Highly-Speeded Test Under Different Instructions Regarding Scoring Penalties." *Educational and Psychological Measurement*, 1963, *23*, 83–99.

Milton, O. *Will That Be on the Final?* Springfield, Ill.: Thomas, 1982.

Milton, O., Pollio, H. R., and Eison, J. A. *Making Sense of College Grades: Why the Grading System Does Not Work and What Can Be Done About It.* San Francisco: Jossey-Bass, 1986.

Milton, O., and Associates. *On College Teaching: A Guide to Contemporary Practices.* San Francisco: Jossey-Bass, 1978.

Murray, J. P. "Better Testing for Better Learning." *College Teaching*, 1990, *38*(4), 148–152.

Natriello, G. "The Impact of Evaluation Processes on Students." *Educational Psychologist*, 1987, *22*, 155–175.

Nitko, A. J. *Educational Tests and Measurement: An Introduction.* Orlando, Fla.: Harcourt Brace Jovanovich, 1983.

Nuss, E. M. "Academic Integrity: Comparing Faculty and Student Attitudes." *College Teaching*, 1984, *32*, 140–144.

Osterling, S. J. *Constructing Test Items.* Boston: Kluwer Academic, 1989.

Pidgeon, D. A., and Yates, A. "Experimental Inquiry into the Use of Essay-Type English Papers." *British Journal of Educational Psychology*, 1957, *27*, 37–47.

Quann, C. J. *Grades and Grading: Historical Perspectives and the 1982 AACRO Study.* Washington, D.C.: American Association of Collegiate Registrars and Admission Officers, 1984.

Ramsden, P. "Student Learning Research: Retrospect and Prospect." *Higher Education Research and Development*, 1985, *4*, 51–69.

Rich, C. E., and Johanson, G. A. "An Item-Level Analysis of 'None of the Above.'" Paper presented at the annual meeting of the American Educational Research Association, Boston, April 1990.

Rigden, J. S., and Tobias, S. "Too Often, College-Level Science Is Dull as Well as Difficult." *The Chronicle of Higher Education,* Mar. 27, 1991, p. A52.

Rogers, E. M. "Examinations: Powerful Agents for Good or Ill in Teaching." *American Journal of Physics,* 1969, *37,* 954–962.

Sabot, R., and Wakeman-Linn, J. "Grade Inflation and Course Choice." *The Journal of Economic Perspectives,* 1991, *5*(1), 159–170.

Sahadeo, D., and Davis, W. E. "Review—Don't Repeat." *College Teaching,* 1988, *36*(3), 111–113.

Saunders, P. *Introduction to Macroeconomics: Student Workbook.* Bloomington, Ind.: Saunders Publishing, 1991.

Semb, G., and Spencer, R. "Beyond the Level of Recall: An Analysis of Higher Order Educational Tasks." In L. Fraley and E. Vargas (eds.), *Proceedings of the Third National Conference on Behavior and Technology in Higher Education.* Atlanta: Georgia State University, 1976.

Sheppard, E. M. "The Effect of Quality of Handwriting on Grades." *Journal of Educational Research,* 1929, *19,* 102–105.

Singhal, A., and Johnson, P. "How to Halt Student Dishonesty." *College Student Journal,* 1983, *17,* 13–19.

Stanley, L. C. "Writing-to-Learn Assignments: The Journal and the Microtheme." In L. C. Stanley and J. Ambron (eds.), *Writing Across the Curriculum in Community Colleges.* New Directions for Community Colleges, no. 73. San Francisco: Jossey-Bass, 1991.

Starch, D., and Elliot, E. C. "Reliability of Grading Work in Mathematics." *School Review,* 1913, *21,* 254–259.

Strauss, M. J., and Clarke, J. H. "Fear and Trembling in the Examination Hour." *Journal of College Science Teaching,* 1989, *18,* 233–235.

Stroud, J. B. *Psychology in Education.* White Plains, N.Y.: Longman, 1946.

"Students Who Take Principles of Sociology from Albert I. McLeod at Cal State University at Fresno Never Ask, 'Will That Be on the Test?'" *The Chronicle of Higher Education,* Dec. 5, 1990, p. A18.

Terwilliger, J. S. "Distinctions Between Item Format and Objectivity in Scoring." Paper presented at the annual meeting of the National Council on Measurement in Education, Chicago, April 1991.

Van den Bergh, H., and Eiting, M. H. "A Method of Estimating Rater Reliability." *Journal of Educational Measurement,* 1989, *26,* 29–40.

Walker, D. F. "What Constitutes Curricular Validity in a High-School-Leaving Examination?" In G. F. Madaus (ed.), *The Courts, Validity and Minimum Competency Testing.* Hingham, Mass.: Kluwer Nijhoff, 1983.

Wesman, A. G. "Writing the Test Item." In R. C. Thorndike (ed.), *Educational Measurement.* Washington, D.C.: American Council on Education, 1971.

Whitney, D. R., and Sabers, D. L. *Improving Essay Examinations: Use of Item Analysis* (Technical Bulletin #11). Iowa City: University of Iowa Evaluation and Examination Service, 1970.

Wise, S. L., and others. "Providing Item Feedback in Computer-Based Tests: Effects of Initial Success and Failure." Paper presented at the annual meeting of the National Council on Measurement in Education, New Orleans, April 1988.

Wolke, R. L. "A Message to Students: 'If You Have a Lawyer Handy, Go Ahead and Cheat Like Crazy.'" *The Chronicle of Higher Education,* May 15, 1991, p. B2.

Index

A

Adaptive testing. *See* Computerized testing
Administration of test, 141–166
All of the above, as an option, 63
Alpha. *See* Coefficient alpha
Alternative assessment procedures, 123–140
Analysis: as cognitive objective, 18–19; measurement of, 21–22
Anxiety. *See* Test anxiety
Application: as cognitive objective, 18–19; measurement of, 21–22

B

Benefits of tests: for faculty, 2–5; for students, 5–7
Bloom's taxonomy. *See* Taxonomy
Bluffing, 118–119

C

Cheating, 152–156; controlling, 153–155; forms of, 153; handling cheating, 155–156
Checklist, in performance testing, 135

Coefficient alpha, 36–37
Cognitive objectives: definition of, 17; student activities and verbs for, 19; taxonomy of, 18–19
Collaborative testing, 129–130; in groups, 129–130; in pairs, 130
Completion items, 95–97
Comprehension: as cognitive objective, 18–19; measurement of, 21–22
Computerized testing, 168–177; adaptive, 170–174; as delivery system, 168–170; test anxiety in, 169; in test laboratories, 174–176
Context-dependent items, 68–69
Correction-for-guessing. *See* Guessing
Correlation, 34–35, 179–181
Course objectives, relationship to instruction and testing, 4–5
Criterion-referenced tests, 10; validity of, 46–47

D

Difficulty. *See* Item difficulty
Directions: for classroom tests, 147–150; importance of, 39, 47; what to include, 147–150
Discrimination, index of, 183–186

229